PEARSON

Dear Medical Terminology Instructor:

It is with great enthusiasm that we introduce you to *Medical Language, 2nd edition* by Susan Turley. The Pearson Health Science team wants to thank you for your support in making *Medical Language* one of the most widely used texts of its kind.

With the groundbreaking launch of the 1st edition in 2006, we learned that students and instructors alike were ready for a change—a change to a dynamic, logically formatted, complete text accompanied by abundant student and instructional resources. In preparing the 2nd edition, we have maintained and refined our approach of immersing students in the language of healthcare. Beyond the book, students will now be able to explore *Medical Terminology Interactive*, an online virtual hospital where they will find quizzes, games, and more to support their studies.

We also wanted to provide you, the instructor, with resources to assist in the immersion process. As with the 1st edition, you will have a multitude of teaching and assessment tools that have been carefully prepared by our author and development team. These tools include a revamped Instructor's Resource Manual packed with worksheets and class assignments, dynamic PowerPoint lectures as well as libraries of images, videos, and tests. And naturally you will have a full range of online learning management options.

In addition, we are now pleased to provide adopters of *Medical Language* with an **Annotated Instructor's Edition (AIE)**. This special printing is exclusively for instructors, as it provides margin notes, tips, ideas, talking points, instructional media links, and bonus content to augment the student edition. Answers to all exercises are also displayed directly on each appropriate page, so there's no need to flip to an appendix. This is your all-in-one resource for facilitating the learning experience. What you are holding in your hands right now is a sample chapter of the AIE. Adopters may request the full version by contacting their Pearson sales representative.

We are confident that you will find *Medical Language, 2nd edition* and its accompanying resources to be the ideal package to prepare your students to speak the language they will use daily in their future careers. So please dig in, dive in, and enjoy your exploration of this revolutionary text!

Sincerely,

Mark Cohen
Editor-in-Chief

Katrin Beacom
Executive Marketing Manager

Pearls of Wisdom

1. Gastroenterology is the study of the entire digestive system and metabolism of nutrients. Nutrition is usually included as a portion of this chapter.

2. A good place to begin teaching any body system is to differentiate between the specialists that treat the structures related to the system. For instance, gastroenterology is a general specialty that treats all organs. That can be seen by deconstructing the term: "gastr" means stomach, "enter" means intestine, and "ology" means the study of. Beginning with the suffix "-ology," the student can readily define the term as study of the stomach and intestines. Obviously, this a broad definition of a complex specialty.

3. Subspecialties include proctology, bariatrics, and colorectal surgeons. Dentistry can also be considered a specialty for the digestive system because the alimentary canal begins with the mouth and teeth. Descriptions of each of these specialties will introduce the student to the basic terminology of this system.

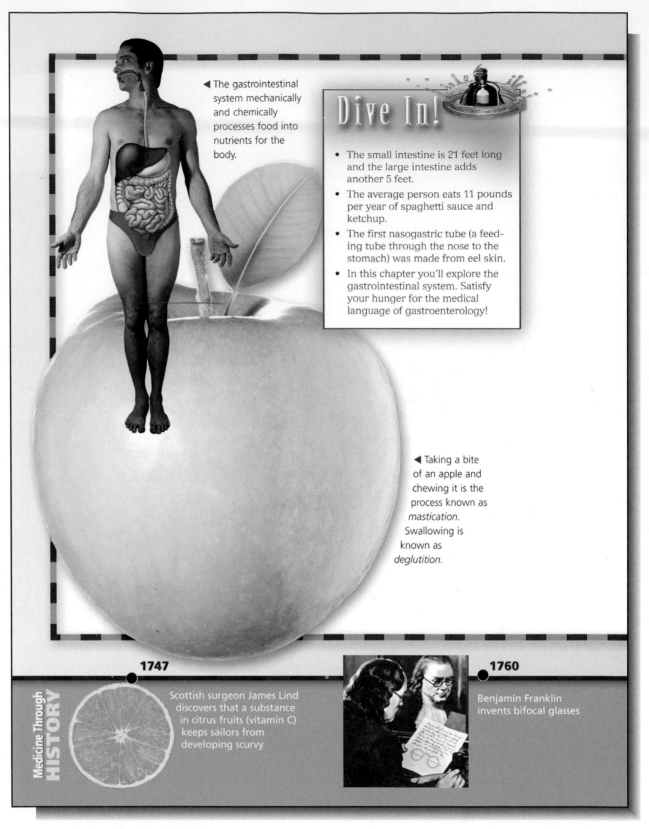

◄ The gastrointestinal system mechanically and chemically processes food into nutrients for the body.

Dive In!

- The small intestine is 21 feet long and the large intestine adds another 5 feet.
- The average person eats 11 pounds per year of spaghetti sauce and ketchup.
- The first nasogastric tube (a feeding tube through the nose to the stomach) was made from eel skin.
- In this chapter you'll explore the gastrointestinal system. Satisfy your hunger for the medical language of gastroenterology!

◄ Taking a bite of an apple and chewing it is the process known as *mastication*. Swallowing is known as *deglutition*.

Medicine Through HISTORY

1747
Scottish surgeon James Lind discovers that a substance in citrus fruits (vitamin C) keeps sailors from developing scurvy

1760
Benjamin Franklin invents bifocal glasses

4. Diagnostic techniques for the gastrointestinal system involve the use of contrast materials, radiology, scopes, and MRI and CT scans. The terminology of such methods should begin by emphasizing the differences between such suffixes as -scope and -scopy, -stomy and -tomy, and -ectomy.

5. Another area to discuss is the accessory organs that are not naturally thought of as part of the digestive system. The alimentary canal is only part of the system. The liver, gallbladder and pancreas are organs that secrete enzymes to assist in digestion and absorption of nutrients.

3
Gastroenterology
Gastrointestinal System

Gastroenterology (GAS-troh-EN-ter-AWL-oh-jee) is the medical specialty that studies the anatomy and physiology of the gastrointestinal system and uses diagnostic tests, medical and surgical procedures, and drugs to treat gastrointestinal diseases.

▶ The sense of taste can detect sweet, salty, sour, bitter, umami (the savory taste of amino acids), fatty acids, and the sensation of metals and water.

1796

Edward Jenner, an English physician, devises the first vaccination by injecting material from cowpox sores to prevent smallpox

1798

John Dalton, an English physicist, describes color blindness

1806

The painkilling drug morphine is isolated from the opium poppy

6. The digestive system is also a system of elimination. Sometimes students will enter the course with little to no knowledge of anatomy. They may not realize that the human body has two systems by which it gets rid of waste products. A brief introduction to the difference between solid waste and liquid waste elimination can help. Explain that the body eliminates liquid waste through the urinary system and solid waste through the intestinal system.

7. Needless to say, spelling should be of major concern to the instructor and students. Recognition of the terms used in context can be accomplished by having the students read operative reports, imaging reports, and scope reports. These reports can be complex but do offer excellent opportunities for learning spelling and contextual use of terms.

Measure Your Progress: Learning Objectives

After you study this chapter, you should be able to

1. Identify the structures of the gastrointestinal system.

2. Describe the process of digestion.

3. Describe common gastrointestinal diseases and conditions, laboratory and diagnostic procedures, medical and surgical procedures, and drug categories.

4. Give the medical meaning of word parts related to the gastrointestinal system.

5. Build gastrointestinal words from word parts and divide and define gastrointestinal words.

6. Spell and pronounce gastrointestinal words.

7. Analyze the medical content and meaning of a gastroenterology report.

8. Dive deeper into gastroenterology by reviewing the activities at the end of this chapter and online at Medical Terminology Interactive.

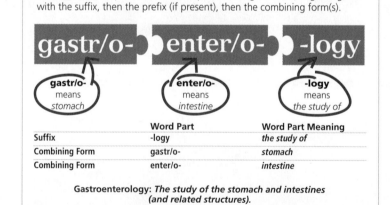

Medical Language Key

To unlock the definition of a medical word, break it into word parts. Define each word part. Put the word part meanings in order, beginning with the suffix, then the prefix (if present), then the combining form(s).

gastr/o- means *stomach*

enter/o- means *intestine*

-logy means *the study of*

	Word Part	Word Part Meaning
Suffix	-logy	*the study of*
Combining Form	gastr/o-	*stomach*
Combining Form	enter/o-	*intestine*

Gastroenterology: *The study of the stomach and intestines (and related structures).*

Figure 3-1 ■ **Gastrointestinal system.**

The gastrointestinal system consists of organs and glands connected in a pathway. Food enters the body, is digested, and undigested wastes are eliminated from the body.

Talking Point

Medical Humor

Young children swallow all kinds of objects, some of which have to be surgically removed. Here's a little joke:

Doctor to nurse: How is that little girl doing who swallowed the 10 quarters last night? Nurse to doctor: No change yet.

Source: Medical jokes, www.ahajokes.com

Anatomy and Physiology

The **gastrointestinal (GI) system** is an elongated body system that begins at the mouth, continues through the thoracic cavity, and fills much of the abdominopelvic cavity (see Figure 3-1 ■). The upper gastrointestinal system includes the structures from the mouth through the stomach. The lower gastrointestinal system includes the structures from the small intestine through the anus. The purpose of the gastrointestinal system is to digest food, absorb nutrients, and remove undigested material (waste) from the body.

WORD BUILDING

gastrointestinal
(GAS-troh-in-TES-tih-nal)
  gastr/o- *stomach*
  intestin/o- *intestine*
  -al *pertaining to*

system (SIS-tem)

Word Alert

The gastrointestinal system is also known as the **gastrointestinal tract,** the **digestive system** or digestive tract, and the **alimentary canal.** Each name highlights a different characteristic of this body system.

1. Tract: a continuing pathway
2. Digestive: describes the purpose of the system
3. Alimentary: refers to food and nourishment
4. Canal: a tubular channel

digestive (dy-JES-tiv)
  digest/o- *break down food;*
    digest
  -ive *pertaining to*

alimentary (AL-ih-MEN-tair-ee)
  aliment/o- *food; nourishment*
  -ary *pertaining to*

Anatomy of the Gastrointestinal System

Oral Cavity and Pharynx

The gastrointestinal system begins in the mouth or **oral cavity** (see Figure 3-2 ■). It contains the teeth, gums, **tongue,** hard **palate,** and soft palate with its fleshy, hanging **uvula.** The oral cavity is lined with **mucosa,** a mucous

oral (OR-al)
  or/o- *mouth*
  -al *pertaining to*
Oral is the adjective form for *mouth.*
The combining form *stomat/o-* also
means *mouth.*

tongue (TUNG)
  lingu/o- *tongue*
  -al *pertaining to*
The combining form *gloss/o-* also
means *tongue.*

palate (PAL-at)

uvula (YOO-vyoo-lah)

mucosa (myoo-KOH-sah)

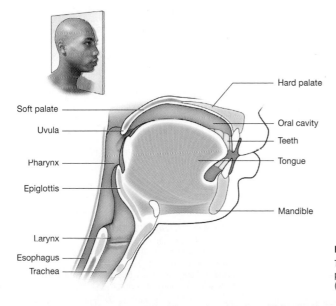

Soft palate
Uvula
Pharynx
Epiglottis
Larynx
Esophagus
Trachea

Hard palate
Oral cavity
Teeth
Tongue
Mandible

Figure 3-2 ■ **Oral cavity and pharynx.**
The oral cavity contains the teeth, gums, tongue, and palate. Food passes from the oral cavity into the pharynx (throat) and then into the esophagus.

TEACHING STRATEGY

Explain the importance of learning the parts of the gastrointestinal system. Students should know the exact path that food takes, starting with the mouth and ending with the anus.

MEDIA RESOURCES

See the PowerPoint presentation on www.myhealthprofessionskit.com for animations and videos on the digestive system.

ETYMOLOGY

Palate comes from a Latin word meaning *roof of the mouth.*

Mucosa is a Latin word meaning *mucus.*

membrane that produces thin mucus. The sense of taste is also associated with the gastrointestinal system. Receptors on the tongue perceive taste and send this information to the **gustatory cortex** in the brain.

The sight, smell, and taste of food cause the salivary glands to release saliva into the mouth. **Saliva** is a lubricant that moistens food as it is chewed and swallowed. Saliva also contains the enzyme amylase that begins the process of digestion. There are three pairs of **salivary glands: the parotid glands, sublingual glands,** and **submandibular glands** (see Figure 3-3 ■).

The teeth tear, chew, and grind food during the process of **mastication.** The tongue moves food toward the teeth and mixes food with saliva. Swallowing or **deglutition** moves food into the throat or pharynx. The **pharynx** is a passageway for food as well as for inhaled and exhaled air. When food is swallowed, the larynx moves upward to close against the epiglottis, so that food in the pharynx does not enter the larynx, trachea, and lungs. If the entrance to the larynx is not closed when food is in the back of the pharynx pressing on the uvula, this initiates the gag reflex.

ETYMOLOGY

Pharynx is a Greek word meaning *throat.*

Across the Life Span

Pediatrics. The first food for many babies is colostrum from the mother's breast. Colostrum is rich in nutrients and contains maternal antibodies. For the first few days of life, the newborn's intestinal tract is permeable and allows these antibodies to be absorbed from the intestine into the blood, where they provide passive immunity to common diseases.

Geriatrics. Older adults often complain that food does not seem as flavorful as when they were younger. The aging process causes a very real decline in the ability to smell and taste food as the number of receptors in the nose and on the tongue decreases.

WORD BUILDING

gustatory (GUS-tah-TOR-ee)
  gustat/o- *the sense of taste*
  -ory *having the function of*

saliva (sah-LY-vah)

salivary (SAL-ih-VAIR-ee)
  saliv/o- *saliva*
  -ary *pertaining to*
The combining form *sial/o-* also means *salivary gland* or *saliva.*

parotid (pah-RAWT-id)
  par- *beside*
  ot/o- *ear*
  -id *resembling; source or origin*

sublingual (sub-LING-gwal)
  sub- *below; underneath; less than*
  lingu/o- *tongue*
  -al *pertaining to*

submandibular
(SUB-man-DIB-yoo-lar)
  sub- *below; underneath; less than*
  mandibul/o- *mandible (lower jaw)*
  -ar *pertaining to*

mastication (MAS-tih-KAY-shun)
  mastic/o- *chewing*
  -ation *a process; being or having*

deglutition (DEE-gloo-TISH-un)
  degluti/o- *swallowing*
  -tion *a process; being or having*

pharynx (FAIR-ingks)

pharyngeal (fah-RIN-jee-al)
  pharyng/o- *pharynx (throat)*
  -eal *pertaining to*

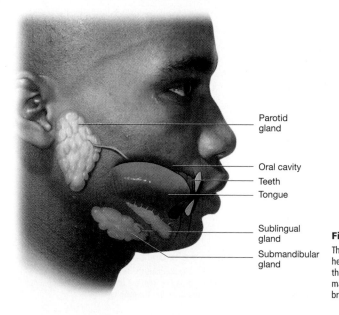

Parotid gland

Oral cavity

Teeth

Tongue

Sublingual gland

Submandibular gland

Figure 3-3 ■ Salivary glands.

The large, flat parotid glands are on either side of the head in front of the ear. The sublingual glands are under the tongue. The submandibular glands are under the mandible (lower jaw bone). Ducts from these glands bring saliva into the oral cavity.

Esophagus

The **esophagus** is a flexible, muscular tube that connects the pharynx to the stomach. It is lined with mucosa that produces mucus. With coordinated contractions of its wall—a process known as **peristalsis**—the esophagus moves food toward the stomach.

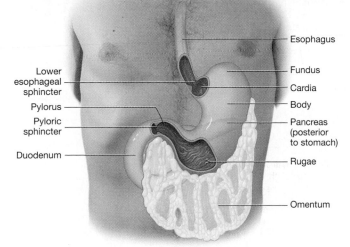

Lower esophageal sphincter
Pylorus
Pyloric sphincter
Duodenum
Esophagus
Fundus
Cardia
Body
Pancreas (posterior to stomach)
Rugae
Omentum

Figure 3-4 ■ Stomach.

The stomach has four regions. The cardia is the small area where the esophagus joins the stomach. The fundus is the rounded top of the stomach. The body is the large, curved part of the stomach. The pylorus is the narrowed canal at the end.

Stomach

The **stomach** (see Figure 3-4 ■) is a large, elongated sac in the upper abdominal cavity. It receives food from the esophagus. The stomach is divided into four regions: the **cardia, fundus, body,** and **pylorus** (see Figure 3-4). The gastric mucosa is arranged in thick, deep folds or **rugae** that expand as the stomach fills with food. The stomach produces hydrochloric acid, pepsinogen, and gastrin to aid in the digestion of food. The mucosa produces mucus that protects the lining of the stomach from the hydrochloric acid.

Two sphincters (muscular rings) keep food in the stomach. The **lower esophageal sphincter (LES)** is located at the distal end of the esophagus. The **pyloric sphincter** is located at the distal end of the stomach. **Chyme** is a semisolid mixture of partially digested food, saliva, digestive enzymes, and fluids in the stomach. An hour or so after eating, the pyloric sphincter opens and waves of peristalsis propel the chyme into the small intestine.

Small Intestine

The **small intestine** or **small bowel** is a long, hollow tube that receives chyme from the stomach. The small intestine produces three digestive enzymes: lactase, maltase, and sucrase. The small intestine consists of three parts: the duodenum, jejunum, and ileum (see Figure 3-5 ■). The

---

WORD BUILDING

esophagus (eh-SAWF-ah-gus)

esophageal (eh-SAWF-ah-JEE-al)
  esophag/o- esophagus
  -eal pertaining to

peristalsis (PAIR-ih-STAL-sis)
  peri- around
  stal/o- contraction
  -sis process; condition; abnormal condition

gastric (GAS-trik)
  gastr/o- stomach
  -ic pertaining to
Gastric is the adjective form for stomach.

cardia (KAR-dee-ah)

fundus (FUN-dus)

pylorus (py-LOR-us)

pyloric (py-LOR-ik)
  pylor/o- pylorus
  -ic pertaining to

rugae (ROO-gee)
The singular form ruga is seldom used.

sphincter (SFINGK-ter)

chyme (KIME)

intestine (in-TES-tin)

intestinal (in-TES-tih-nal)
  intestin/o- intestine
  -al pertaining to
The combining form enter/o- also means intestine.

ETYMOLOGY

Cardia comes from a Greek word meaning *heart*. The cardia of the stomach and the cardiac sphincter of the esophagus are near to, but not part of, the heart.

Fundus is a Latin word meaning *upper part that is the farthest from the lower opening.*

Ruga is a Latin singular feminine noun meaning *wrinkle.*

Sphincter comes from a Greek word meaning *bind up tightly.*

The Latin combining form *rect/o-* means *rectum,* but so does the Greek combining form *proct/o-.* The Greek form was used in the past (but seldom now) in such words as *proctitis* and *proctologist.*

Activities

Memory Aids

Memory aids or "nnifty mnemonic devices" help you remember the order of the anatomical structures of the gastrointestinal system. These memory aids were created by students.

■ To remember the parts of the colon (Ascending, transverse, descending, sigmoid) use this memory aid: All things down south.

■ To remember the parts of the small intestine (duodenum; jejunum, ileum) use either of these memory aids:

Dogs eat junk and don't get ill   Dow Jones Industrial

■ To remember the parts of the large intestine (cecum, colon, rectum, anus) use either of these memory aids:

Cats eat canaries and run away   Call Cal Ripkin awesome

duodenum is a 10-inch, C-shaped segment that begins at the stomach and ends at the jejunum. Digestive enzymes from the gallbladder and pancreas flow through ducts into the duodenum. The **jejunum,** the second part of the small intestine, is an 8-foot segment that repeatedly twists and turns in the abdominal cavity. Digestion continues in the jejunum. Peristalsis slowly moves the chyme along for several hours until it reaches the ileum, the final part of the small intestine. The **ileum** is a 12-foot segment where absorption of nutrients is completed. The ileum contains **villi,** thousands of small, thin structures that project into the **lumen** (central, open area) and increase the amount of surface area to maximize the absorption of food nutrients and water through the intestinal wall and into the blood. The remaining undigested material (waste) and water move into the large intestine.

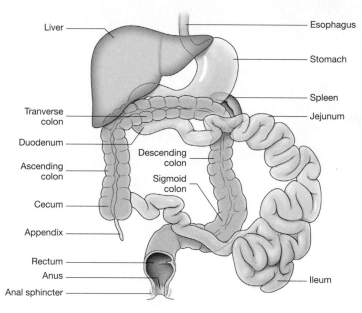

Figure 3-5 ■ Small and large intestines.
The small intestine consists of the duodenum, jejunum, and ileum. The large intestine consists of the cecum (and appendix), colon, rectum, and anus. The colon can be divided into the ascending colon, transverse colon, descending colon, and sigmoid colon. The bends (flexures) in the colon are landmarks that are mentioned in x-ray reports. The bend near the liver is the hepatic flexure. The bend near the spleen is the splenic flexure.

Large Intestine

The **large intestine** or **large bowel** is a larger, hollow tube that receives undigested material and some water from the small intestine. The large intestine consists of the cecum, colon, rectum, and anus (see Figure 3-5). The **cecum** is a short sac. Hanging from its external wall is the **appendix,** a thin tube that is closed at its distal end.

The walls of the large intestine contain **haustra** (puckered pouches) that can greatly expand as needed. Waves of peristalsis slowly move undigested material through the large intestine as water is absorbed through the intestinal wall and into the blood.

Activity

Demonstration

Bring something to class to demonstrate the total length of the small and large intestines: thin rope, string, beads, etc. Have the students stand around the room and each hold a segment of the total length.

The **colon** is the longest part of the large intestine. It travels through all four quadrants of the abdomen as the **ascending colon, transverse colon, descending colon,** and **sigmoid colon** (see Figure 3-5). As the ascending colon nears the liver, it bends in a right angle at the hepatic flexure. As the transverse colon nears the spleen, it bends in a right angle at the splenic flexure. The sigmoid colon bends toward the midline in an S-shaped curve that joins the rectum. The **rectum** is a short, straight segment that connects to the outside of the body. The **anus,** the external opening of the rectum, is located between the buttocks. The anal sphincter is a muscular ring whose opening and closing is under conscious, voluntary control.

Did You Know?

The appendix or vermiform appendix can be up to 8 inches in length. *Vermiform* is a Latin word meaning *wormlike*. The appendix plays no role in digestion. It is part of the lymphatic system and the immune response (discussed in "Hematology and Immunology," Chapter 6).

Clinical Connections

Immunology (Chapter 6). Some parts of the gastrointestinal system are also part of the body's immune response. Saliva contains antibodies that destroy microorganisms in the food we eat. Small areas on the walls of the intestines (Peyer's patches) and in the appendix contain white blood cells that destroy microorganisms. However, ingested microorganisms can still cause gastrointestinal illness.

Abdomen and Abdominopelvic Cavity

The anterior **abdominal wall** can be divided into four quadrants or nine regions (discussed in "The Body in Health and Disease," Chapter 2).

The **abdominopelvic cavity** contains the largest organs (viscera) of the gastrointestinal system. The **peritoneum** is a double-layer serous membrane. One layer lines the walls of the abdominopelvic cavity. The other layer surrounds each of the organs. The peritoneum secretes **peritoneal fluid,** a watery fluid that fills the spaces between the organs and allows them to slide past each other during the movements of digestion.

The peritoneum extends into the center of the abdominopelvic cavity as the **omentum** (see Figure 3-4). The omentum supports the stomach and hangs down as a fatty apron to cover and protect the small intestine. The peritoneum also extends as the **mesentery,** a thick, fan-shaped sheet that supports the jejunum and ileum.

The blood supply to the stomach, small intestine, liver, gallbladder, and pancreas comes from the **celiac trunk** of the abdominal aorta, the largest artery in the body.

Accessory Organs of Digestion

The liver, gallbladder, and pancreas are accessory organs of digestion. They contribute to, but are not physically involved in, the process of digestion.

WORD BUILDING

colon (KOH-lon)

colonic (koh-LAWN-ik)
  colon/o- *colon*
  -ic *pertaining to*
The combining form *col/o-* also means *colon.*

sigmoid (SIG-moyd)
The combining form *sigmoid/o-* means *sigmoid colon.*

rectum (REK-tum)

rectal (REK-tal)
  rect/o- *rectum*
  -al *pertaining to*
The combining form *proct/o-* also means *rectum.*

anus (AA-nus)

anal (AA-nal)
  an/o- *anus*
  -al *pertaining to*

abdominal (ab-DAWM-ih-nal)
  abdomin/o- *abdomen*
  -al *pertaining to*
The combining forms *celi/o-* and *lapar/o-* also mean *abdomen.*

abdominopelvic
(ab-DAWM-ih-noh-PEL-vik)
  abdomin/o- *abdomen*
  pelv/o- *pelvis (hip bone; renal pelvis)*
  -ic *pertaining to*

peritoneum (PAIR-ih-toh-NEE-um)

peritoneal (PAIR-ih-toh-NEE-al)
  peritone/o- *peritoneum*
  -al *pertaining to*
The combining form *periton/o-* also means *peritoneum.*

omentum (oh-MEN-tum)

mesentery (MEZ-en-TAIR-ee)

mesenteric (MEZ-en-TAIR-ik)
  meso- *middle*
  enter/o- *intestine*
  -ic *pertaining to*
Delete the *o-* on *meso-* before building the word.

celiac (SEE-lee-ak)
  celi/o- *abdomen*
  -ac *pertaining to*

ETYMOLOGY

Sigmoid combines the word *sigma* (the Greek letter S) and the suffix *-oid* (resembling). The curving shape of the sigmoid colon resembles the letter *S*.

Rectum comes from a Latin word meaning *straight*. The rectum is the straight segment after the curving sigmoid colon.

Anus is a Latin word meaning *circle*.

DID YOU KNOW?

- Up to 80 percent of the human liver can be removed without causing death. The remaining 20 percent will regenerate.
- The mesentery is only attached to the middle of the small intestine.

ETYMOLOGY

Peritoneum is a Latin word meaning *stretched around*.

Omentum is a Latin word meaning *membrane that encloses the bowels*.

Talking Point

Computer Analogy

If you are over age 40, try to remember the first time someone talked to you about computers. You probably heard the words "mouse," "bites," and "windows." These words were familiar to you, but the meanings that you knew were incorrect in the context of computers. This is how it is with medical language. From your own living experience, you probably already have an idea as to the meanings of the words "gynecology" or "gastritis," but you may not know the correct or full meaning of these words.

ETYMOLOGY

Hepatic is the adjective form for *liver*.

In *bilirubin*, the combining form *rub/o-* means *red*. Old red blood cells break down and release bilirubin that is incorporated into bile by the liver.

In *biliverdin*, the combining form *verd/o-* means *green* and the suffix *-in* means *a substance*.

The combining form for *gallbladder* is in medical words pertaining to diseases and surgeries of the gallbladder. Cholecystokinin moves (stimulates) the gallbladder and pancreas.

Pancreas comes from a Greek word meaning *sweetbread*. The pancreas of a large animal was considered a culinary delicacy.

DID YOU KNOW?

More than 500 strains of bacteria live in the human mouth.

The **liver,** a large, dark red-brown organ, is located in the upper abdomen (see Figure 3-6 ■). Liver cells **(hepatocytes)** continuously produce **bile,** a yellow-green, bitter-tasting, thick fluid. Bile is a combination of bile acids, mucus, fluid, and two pigments: the yellow pigment **bilirubin** and the green pigment **biliverdin.** Bile produced by the liver flows through the common hepatic duct and into the common bile duct to the duodenum. When the duct is full, bile flows into the cystic duct and gallbladder. All of the **bile ducts** collectively are known as the **biliary tree.**

The **gallbladder** is a teardrop-shaped, dark green sac posterior to the liver (see Figure 3-6). It concentrates and stores bile from the liver. The presence of fatty chyme in the duodenum causes the gallbladder to contract, sending bile into the common bile duct and then into the duodenum to digest fats.

The **pancreas** is a yellow, somewhat lumpy gland shaped like an elongated triangle (see Figure 3-6). It is located posterior to the stomach. The presence of food in the duodenum causes the pancreas to secrete digestive enzymes (amylase, lipase, and others) through the pancreatic duct and into the duodenum. The pancreas also functions as an organ of the endocrine system (discussed in "Endocrinology," Chapter 14).

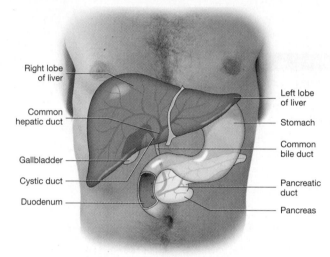

Right lobe of liver
Common hepatic duct
Gallbladder
Cystic duct
Duodenum
Left lobe of liver
Stomach
Common bile duct
Pancreatic duct
Pancreas

Figure 3-6 ■ Biliary tree.

Bile flows through hepatic ducts in the liver that merge to form the common hepatic duct. It joins the cystic duct from the gallbladder to form the common bile duct. Because of their appearance, these ducts are known as the biliary tree. The pancreatic duct joins the common bile duct just before it enters the duodenum.

Physiology of Digestion

The process of **digestion** begins in the oral cavity (see Figure 3-7 ■). There are two parts to digestion: mechanical and chemical.

Mechanical digestion uses mastication (tearing, crushing, and grinding of food in the mouth), deglutition (swallowing), and peristalsis (mixing and moving a bolus of food through the esophagus, and mixing and moving chyme and undigested material through the stomach and intestines). Mechanical digestion also involves breaking apart fats in the duodenum. Fatty

WORD BUILDING

liver (LIV-er)

hepatic (heh-PAT-ik)
　hepat/o- *liver*
　-ic *pertaining to*

hepatocyte (HEP-ah-TOH-site)
　hepat/o- *liver*
　-cyte *cell*

bile (BILE)
The combining forms *bili/o-* and *chol/e-* mean *bile* or *gall*.

bilirubin (BIL-ih-ROO-bin)

biliverdin (BIL-ih-VER-din)

bile duct (BILE DUKT)
The combining form *cholangi/o-* means *bile duct*. The combining form *choledoch/o-* means *common bile duct*.

biliary (BIL-ee-AIR-ee)
　bili/o- *bile; gall*
　-ary *pertaining to*

gallbladder (GAWL-blad-er)
The combining form *cholecyst/o-* means *gallbladder*.

pancreas (PAN-kree-as)

pancreatic (PAN-kree-AT-ik)
　pancreat/o- *pancreas*
　-ic *pertaining to*

digestion (dy-JES-chun) (dih-JES-chun)
　digest/o- *break down food; digest*
　-ion *action; condition*

chyme stimulates the duodenum to secrete the hormone **cholecystokinin,** which stimulates the gallbladder to contract and release bile. Bile breaks apart large globules of fat during the process of **emulsification.**

Chemical digestion uses **enzymes** and acid to break down foods. The enzyme amylase in saliva begins to break down carbohydrate foods in the mouth. The stomach secretes the following substances that continue the process of chemical digestion.

- **Hydrochloric acid (HCl).** This strong acid breaks down food fibers, converts pepsinogen to the digestive enzyme pepsin, and kills microorganisms in food.
- **Pepsinogen.** This inactive substance is converted by hydrochloric acid to **pepsin,** a digestive enzyme that breaks down protein foods into large protein molecules.
- **Gastrin.** This hormone stimulates the release of more hydrochloric acid and pepsinogen.

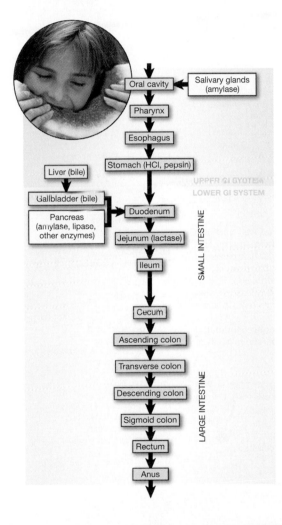

Figure 3-7 ■ **Gastrointestinal system.**
Everyone enjoys eating! The gastrointestinal system helps you taste and enjoy the food you eat and then uses mechanical and chemical means to break down that food into nutrients that nourish your body.

WORD BUILDING

cholecystokinin
(KOH-lee-sis-toh-KY-nin)
  cholecyst/o- *gallbladder*
  kin/o- *movement*
  -in *a substance*

emulsification
(ee-MUL-sih-tih-KAY-shun)
  emulsific/o- *droplets of fat*
    suspended in a liquid
  -ation *a process; being or having*

enzyme (EN-zime)

hydrochloric acid
(HY-droh-KLOR-ik AS-id)
  hydr/o- *water; fluid*
  chlor/o- *chloride*
  -ic *pertaining to*

pepsinogen (pep-SIN-oh-jen)
  pepsin/o- *pepsin*
  -gen *that which produces*

pepsin (PEP-sin)
  peps/o- *digestion*
  -in *a substance*

gastrin (GAS-trin)
  gastr/o- *stomach*
  -in *a substance*

ETYMOLOGY

Enzyme is a Greek word meaning *leaven.* Enzymes speed up chemical reactions just as leaven (yeast) speeds up the rising of bread.

DID YOU KNOW?

- The masseter muscle that chews food is the strongest muscle in the body. It can generate up to 200 pounds of pressure on the teeth.

  Source: Fun Science Facts, www.hightech science.org/ funfacts.htm

- The body produces about a quart of saliva each day and about 10,000 gallons over a lifetime.

  Source: Fun Science Facts, www.hightech science.org/ funfacts.htm

Activity

Bedside Commode

If you are a particularly fearless instructor and your college has a medical assisting or nursing department, you might want to borrow a bedside commode—and deliver this part of your lecture while sitting on it (with the lid closed, of course!).

The popularized "taste map of the tongue" is incorrect. All regions of the tongue can detect different tastes such as bitter, sweet, salty, and sour. A newer taste known as unami is a savory taste such as in meat and soy sauce.

Chemical digestion continues in the small intestine as cholecystokinin from the duodenum also stimulates the pancreas to secrete its digestive enzymes into the duodenum.

- **Amylase** continues the digestion of carbohydrates that was begun by amylase in the saliva. It breaks down carbohydrates and starches into sugars and food fibers.
- **Lipase** breaks down small fat globules into fatty acids.
- Other enzymes break down large protein molecules into peptide chains and then break down peptide chains into amino acids.

The villi of the small intestine produce digestive enzymes such as **lactase** to break down sugars. The simple sugar glucose is the only source of energy that body cells can use.

Clinical Connections

Hematology (Chapter 6). The stomach plays an indirect role in the production of red blood cells. It secretes intrinsic factor that allows vitamin B_{12} (a building block of red blood cells) to be absorbed from the intestine into the blood. When the stomach does not produce enough intrinsic factor or when part of the stomach is removed (gastrectomy) because of a cancerous tumor, vitamin B_{12} is not absorbed; the red blood cells that are formed are very large, fragile, and die prematurely. This disease is called pernicious anemia.

Dietetics. Individuals whose small intestine does not produce enough of the digestive enzyme lactase experience gas and bloating when they drink milk or eat dairy products. This is caused by undigested lactose (the sugar in milk).

WORD BUILDING

amylase (AM-il-ace)
   amyl/o- *carbohydrate; starch*
   -ase *enzyme*

lipase (LIP-ace)
   lip/o- *lipid (fat)*
   -ase *enzyme*

lactase (LAK-tace)
   lact/o- *milk*
   -ase *enzyme*

ETYMOLOGY

Elimination comes from a Latin word meaning *to throw something out the door.*

Feces comes from a Latin word meaning *the dregs.*

Stool comes from an English word meaning *a seat with legs but no arms or back.* It then came to mean *a toilet* and then *waste expelled from the body.*

Flatus is a Latin word meaning *blowing.*

Absorption of nutrients and water through the intestinal wall and into the blood takes place in the small intestine, while absorption of any remaining water takes place in the large intestine. Absorbed nutrients are carried in the blood of a large vein that goes to the liver. The liver plays an important role in regulating nutrients such as glucose and amino acids. Excess glucose in the blood is stored in the liver as glycogen and released when the blood glucose level is low. The liver uses amino acids to build plasma proteins and clotting factors for the blood.

Elimination occurs when undigested materials and water are eliminated from the body in a solid waste form known as **feces** or **stool**. The process of elimination is a bowel movement or **defecation.**

A Closer Look

The large intestine is inhabited by millions of beneficial bacteria that produce vitamin K to supplement what is in the diet. These bacteria also change the yellow-green pigment in bile to the characteristic brown color of feces. Bacteria in the large intestine feed on undigested materials and produce intestinal gas or **flatus.**

absorption (ab-SORP-shun)
   absorpt/o- *absorb; take in*
   -ion *action; condition*

elimination (ee-LIM-ih-NAY-shun)
The combining form *chez/o-* means *to pass feces.*

feces (FEE-seez)

fecal (FEE-kal)
   fec/o- *feces; stool*
   -al *pertaining to*
The combining form *fec/a-* also means *feces.*

stool (STOOL)

defecation (DEF-eh-KAY-shun)
   de- *reversal of; without*
   fec/o- *feces; stool*
   -ation *a process; being or having*

flatus (FLAY-tus)

Activity

Digestion Sequence

To learn the process of digestion, give each student an individual sticky note that has an anatomical structure written on it. Have students arrange themselves in anatomical order to show the pathway that food takes from entering the body to being excreted.

Talking Point

Snakes Alive!

When you think of the esophagus, think of a long snake that has swallowed food and you can actually see the bolus (bulge) of food slowly moving down the snake because of peristalsis.

Source: Carol Rinzler, *Nutrition for Dummies.* Foster City, CA: IDA Books, 1997.

Vocabulary Review

Anatomy and Physiology

Word or Phrase	Description	Combining Forms
alimentary canal	Alternate name for the gastrointestinal system	aliment/o- food; nourishment
digestive system	Alternate name for the gastrointestinal system. It is also known as the digestive tract.	digest/o- break down food; digest
gastrointestinal system	Body system that includes the salivary glands, oral cavity (teeth, gums, palate, and tongue), pharynx, esophagus, stomach, small and large intestines, and the accesssory organs of the liver, gallbladder, and pancreas. Its function is to digest food, absorb nutrients into the blood, and remove undigested material from the body. It is also known as the gastrointestinal tract, digestive tract or system, and alimentary canal.	gastr/o- stomach intestin/o- intestine

Oral Cavity and Pharynx

Word or Phrase	Description	Combining Forms
deglutition	Process of swallowing food	degluti/o- swallowing
gustatory cortex	Area of the brain that receives and interprets tastes from the tongue	gustat/o- the sense of taste
mastication	Process of chewing. This is part of the process of mechanical digestion.	mastic/o- chewing
mucosa	Mucous membrane that lines the gastrointestinal system and produces mucus	
oral cavity	Mouth. Hollow area that contains the hard palate, soft palate, uvula, tongue, gums, and teeth	or/o- mouth stomat/o- mouth
palate	The hard bone and posterior soft tissues that form the roof of the mouth	
pharynx	Throat. The passageway for both food and inhaled and exhaled air	pharyng/o- pharynx (throat)
salivary glands	Three pairs of glands (parotid, submandibular, and sublingual) that secrete saliva into the mouth. Saliva is a watery substance that contains the digestive enzyme amylase.	saliv/o- saliva sial/o- saliva ot/o- ear mandibul/o- mandible (lower jaw) lingu/o- tongue
tongue	Large muscle that fills the oral cavity and assists with eating and talking. It contains receptors for the sense of taste.	lingu/o- tongue gloss/o- tongue
uvula	Fleshy hanging part of the soft palate. It plays a role in speech and, during swallowing, it initiates the gag reflex to prevent food from entering the pharynx before the epiglottis closes over the larynx.	

Esophagus and Stomach

Word or Phrase	Description	Combining Forms
cardia	Small area where the esophagus enters the stomach	
chyme	Partially digested food, saliva, and digestive enzymes in the stomach and small intestine	
esophagus	Flexible, muscular tube that moves food from the pharynx to the stomach	esophag/o- esophagus

Activity

Breaking Down Carbohydrates

Bring to class some Hunt Club or Ritz crackers, one for each student. Have students brush off the salt on the top of the cracker, place it in the mouth, and let it dissolve slowly. At some point, there will be a slight sweet taste. This occurs when the amylase in the saliva has broken down the starch (complex carbohydrate) in the cracker into simple sugar. As students swallow, have them place their hand on their anterior throat. Ask, "what is the structure that moves when you swallow?" [larynx or voice box, also known as the Adam's apple] Tell students that the larynx must move upwards in order to close against the stationary epiglottis. The epiglottis acts as a lid to seal the opening of the larynx. Otherwise, the cracker they swallowed would have gone into the larynx and lungs instead of into the esophagus and stomach!

Activity

Medical Terminology Bee

Create a PowerPoint presentation with combining forms, prefixes, and suffixes with their meanings. Use this presentation in class. All students participate in a medical terminology bee. All students stand and take turns defining the combining form, prefix, or suffix displayed. If the student gets the answer right, the student remains standing and continues to play. If the student gets the answer wrong, the student will be seated and is out of the game. The last person standing is the winner. A prize could be given to the winner.

Word or Phrase	Description	Combining Forms
fundus	Rounded, most superior part of the stomach	
lower esophageal sphincter (LES)	Muscular ring at the distal end of the esophagus. It keeps food in the stomach from going back into the esophagus.	esophag/o- *esophagus*
peristalsis	Contractions of smooth muscle that propel a bolus of food, and then chyme, waste products, and water through the gastrointestinal tract	stal/o- *contraction*
pyloric sphincter	Muscular ring that keeps chyme in the stomach or opens to let chyme into the duodenum	pylor/o- *pylorus*
pylorus	Narrowing area of the stomach just before it joins the duodenum. It contains the pyloric sphincter.	pylor/o- *pylorus*
rugae	Deep folds in the gastric mucosa that expand to accommodate food	
stomach	Organ of digestion between the esophagus and the small intestine. Areas of the stomach: cardia, fundus, body, and pylorus. The stomach secretes hydrochloric acid, pepsinogen, and gastrin. The stomach secretes intrinsic factor needed to absorb vitamin B_{12}.	gastr/o- *stomach*

Small and Large Intestines

Word or Phrase	Description	Combining Forms
anus	External opening of the rectum. The external anal sphincter is under voluntary control.	an/o- *anus*
appendix	Long, thin pouch on the exterior wall of the cecum. It does not play a role in digestion. It contains lymphatic tissue and is active in the body's immune response.	appendic/o- *appendix* append/o- *appendix*
cecum	Short, pouch-like first part of the large intestine. The appendix is attached to the cecum's external wall.	cec/o- *cecum*
colon	Longest part of the large intestine. It consists of the **ascending colon, transverse colon, descending colon,** and S-shaped **sigmoid colon.**	col/o- *colon* colon/o- *colon* sigmoid/o- *sigmoid colon*
duodenum	First part of the small intestine. It secretes the hormone cholecystokinin. Digestion takes place there, as well as some absorption of nutrients and water.	duoden/o- *duodenum*
haustra	Pouches in the wall of the large intestine that expand to accommodate the bulk of undigested materials	
ileum	Third part of the small intestine. It connects to the cecum of the large intestine. Some digestion takes place there. There is absorption of nutrients and water through the wall of the ileum and into the blood.	ile/o- *ileum*
jejunum	Second part of the small intestine. Digestion takes place there, as well as some absorption of nutrients and water through the intestinal wall and into the blood.	jejun/o- *jejunum*
large intestine	Organ of absorption between the small intestine and the anus. The large intestine includes the cecum, colon, rectum, and anus. It is also known as the **large bowel.**	intestin/o- *intestine*

Activity

Study Aid

Have students make flashcards for all of the prefixes, suffixes, and combining forms in the chapter. An index card makes a good homemade flashcard. One side of the flashcard should contain the word part and the other side should contain the meaning of the word part. Flashcards can also be printed from the student media. Tell students that flashcards can be carried everywhere and reviewed while waiting for a doctor's appointment, waiting for the bus, etc. Students can recruit family members, especially children, to help them study their flashcards.

As an additional self-quiz, tell students to first look at the meaning of the word part and then remember what the word part is.

Word or Phrase	Description	Combining Forms
lumen	Open channel inside a tubular structure such as the esophagus, small intestine, and large intestine	
rectum	Final part of the large intestine. It is a short, straight segment that lies between the sigmoid colon and the anus.	rect/o- *rectum* proct/o- *rectum*
small intestine	Organ of digestion between the stomach and the large intestine. The duodenum, jejunum, and ileum are the three parts of the small intestine. It is also known as the **small bowel.**	intestin/o- *intestine* enter/o- *intestine*
villi	Microscopic projections of the mucosa in the small intestine. They produce digestive enzymes such as lactase to break down sugars. They have a very large combined surface area to maximize the absorption of nutrients into the blood.	

Abdomen, Liver, Gallbladder, and Pancreas

abdominopelvic cavity	Continuous cavity within the **abdomen** and pelvis that contains the largest organs (viscera) of the gastrointestinal system	abdomin/o- *abdomen* celi/o- *abdomen* lapar/o- *abdomen* pelv/o- *pelvis (hip bone; renal pelvis)*
bile	Bitter fluid produced by the liver and stored in the gallbladder. It is released into the duodenum to digest the fat in foods. It contains the green pigment biliverdin and the yellow pigment bilirubin.	bili/o- *bile; gall* chol/e- *bile; gall*
bile ducts	Bile produced by the liver flows through the hepatic ducts to the common hepatic duct. Then it goes into the common bile duct to the duodenum. When that duct is full, bile goes into the cystic duct and gallbladder. All of these ducts form the **biliary tree,** a treelike structure.	bili/o- *bile; gall* cholangi/o- *bile duct* choledoch/o- *common bile duct*
celiac trunk	Part of the abdominal aorta where arteries branch off to take blood to the stomach, small intestine, liver, gallbladder, and pancreas	celi/o- *abdomen*
gallbladder	Small, dark green sac posterior to the liver that stores and concentrates bile. When stimulated by cholecystokinin from the duodenum, it contracts and releases bile into the common bile duct to the duodenum.	cholecyst/o- *gallbladder*
liver	Largest solid organ in the body. It contains **hepatocytes** that produce bile.	hepat/o- *liver*
mesentery	Thick sheet of peritoneum that supports the jejunum and ileum	enter/o- *intestine*
omentum	Broad, fatty apron of peritoneum. It supports the stomach and protects the small intestine.	
pancreas	Triangular organ located posterior to the stomach. It secretes digestive enzymes (amylase, lipase, and other enzymes) into the duodenum.	pancreat/o- *pancreas*
peritoneum	Double-layer serous membrane that lines the abdominopelvic cavity and surrounds each gastrointestinal organ. It secretes peritoneal fluid to fill the spaces between the organs.	peritone/o- *peritoneum* periton/o- *peritoneum*

Activity

Demonstration

Have students use water-soluble markers to draw the parts of the gastrointestinal system from the esophagus to the large intestine on a willing family member (spouse or child). Have them outline the edges of each organ or structure and then insert the first letter within it: Example: Draw a tubular shaped, vertical structure for the esophagus and write an "E" for "esophagus" in the center. That way, the sight of the "E" on the skin of the neck can be easily recalled and the word "esophagus" will come to mind. Tell students to take a photograph and show it to you.

Digestion

Word or Phrase	Description	Combining Forms
absorption	Process by which digested nutrients move through villi of the small intestine and into the blood	**absorpt/o-** *absorb; take in*
amylase	Digestive enzyme in saliva that begins digestion of carbohydrates in the mouth. It is also secreted by the pancreas to finish the digestion of carbohydrates in the small intestine.	**amyl/o-** *carbohydrate; starch*
cholecystokinin	Hormone secreted by the duodenum when it receives fatty chyme from the stomach. Cholecystokinin stimulates the gallbladder to release bile and the pancreas to release its digestive enzymes.	**cholecyst/o-** *gallbladder* **kin/o-** *movement*
defecation	Process by which undigested materials and water are removed from the body as a bowel movement	**fec/o-** *feces; stool*
digestion	Process of mechanically and chemically breaking down food into nutrients that can be used by the body	**digest/o-** *break down food; digest*
elimination	Process in which undigested materials and water are eliminated from the body	**chez/o-** *to pass feces*
emulsification	Process in which bile breaks down large fat droplets into smaller droplets	**emulsific/o-** *droplets of fat suspended in a liquid*
enzymes	Proteins that speed up chemical reactions in the body. During chemical digestion, enzymes break the chemical bonds in large food molecules. Enzymes are produced by the salivary glands, stomach, small intestine, and pancreas. An enzyme name usually ends in *-ase.*	
feces	Formed, solid waste composed of undigested material, bacteria, and water that is eliminated from the body. It is also known as **stool.**	**fec/a-** *feces; stool* **fec/o-** *feces; stool*
flatus	Gas produced by bacteria that inhabit the large intestine	
gastrin	Hormone produced by the stomach. It stimulates the release of hydrochloric acid and pepsinogen in the stomach.	**gastr/o-** *stomach*
hydrochloric acid	Strong acid produced by the stomach. It breaks down food, kills microorganisms in food, and converts pepsinogen to pepsin.	**chlor/o-** *chloride* **hydr/o-** *water; fluid*
lactase	Digestive enzyme from villi in the small intestine. It breaks down lactose, the sugar in milk.	**lact/o-** *milk*
lipase	Digestive enzyme secreted by the pancreas. It breaks down fat globules in the duodenum into fatty acids.	**lip/o-** *lipid (fat)*
pepsin	Digestive enzyme in the stomach that breaks down protein foods into large protein molecules.	**peps/o-** *digestion*
pepsinogen	Inactive substance produced by the stomach that is converted by hydrochloric acid to the digestive enzyme pepsin.	**pepsin/o-** *pepsin*

Activity

Study Aid

Instruct students to watch CSI, ER, or another medical show. Have students write down examples of three medical words (preferably from this chapter) and the sentences in which they were used in the show. Tell them to be sure to spell the words correctly and write their definitions.

Activity

Study Aid

Tell students to keep a running list in their notebook of sound-alike words or combining forms that have the same meanings. Tell them to title this list of challenging words and word parts as "Perplexing Pairs." Have them begin by writing down the words or word parts found in the Word Alert boxes in this chapter. Then they should add the word parts found in the It's Greek to Me box at the end of this chapter.) Have them add any other words or word parts that they found particularly confusing. Have them add to this list as they complete each chapter. Examples:

orth/o-	vs.	arthr/o-	myel/o-	vs.	my/o-
perine/o-	vs.	peritone/o-	cephal/o-	vs.	encephal/o-

Labeling Exercise

Match each anatomy word or phrase to its structure and write it in the numbered box for each figure. Be sure to check your spelling. Use the Answer Key at the end of the book to check your answers.

| esophagus | parotid gland | sublingual gland | teeth |
| oral cavity | pharynx | submandibular gland | tongue |

1. oral cavity
2. tongue
3. teeth
4. submandibular gland
5. sublingual gland
6. parotid gland
7. pharynx
8. esophagus

body of stomach	esophagus	omentum	pylorus
cardia	fundus	pancreas	rugae
duodenum	lower esophageal sphincter	pyloric sphincter	

1. esophagus
2. lower esophageal sphincter
3. pancreas
4. pyloric sphincter
5. pylorus
6. duodenum
7. rugae
8. fundus
9. cardia
10. body of stomach
11. omoentum

anus	descending colon	jejunum	sigmoid colon
appendix	duodenum	liver	sphincter, anal
ascending colon	gallbladder	pancreas	stomach
cecum	ileum	rectum	transverse colon

1.   liver

2.   gallbladder

3.   pancreas

4.   duodenum

5.   ascending colon

6.   transverse colon

7.   descending colon

8.   cecum

9.   appendix

10.   rectum

11.   sphincter, anal

12.   stomach

13.   jejunum

14.   ileum

15.   sigmoid colon

16.   anus

Building Medical Words

Use the Answer Key at the end of the book to check your answers.

Combining Forms Exercise

Before you build gastrointestinal words, review these combining forms. Next to each combining form, write its medical meaning. The first one has been done for you.

Combining Form	Medical Meaning	Combining Form	Medical Meaning
1. **hydr/o-**	water; fluid	30. gustat/o-	the sense of taste
2. abdomin/o-	abdomen	31. hepat/o-	liver
3. absorpt/o-	absorb; take in	32. ile/o-	ileum (third part of small intestine)
4. aliment/o-	food; nourishment	33. intestin/o-	intestine
5. amyl/o-	carbohydrate; starch	34. jejun/o-	jejunum (middle part of small intestine)
6. an/o-	anus	35. kin/o-	movement
7. appendic/o-	appendix	36. lact/o-	milk
8. append/o-	small structure hanging from a larger structure; appendix	37. lapar/o-	abdomen
9. bili/o-	bile; gall	38. lingu/o-	tongue
10. cec/o-	cecum (first part of large intestine)	39. lip/o-	lipid (fat)
11. celi/o-	abdomen	40. mandibul/o-	mandible (lower jaw)
12. chez/o-	to pass feces	41. mastic/o-	chewing
13. chlor/o-	chloride	42. or/o-	mouth
14. cholangi/o-	bile duct	43. ot/o-	ear
15. chol/e-	bile; gall	44. pancreat/o-	pancreas
16. cholecyst/o-	gallbladder	45. pelv/o-	pelvis (hip bone; renal pelvis)
17. choledoch/o-	common bile duct	46. peps/o-	digestion
18. col/o-	colon (part of large intestine)	47. pepsin/o-	pepsin
19. colon/o-	colon (part of large intestine)	48. peritone/o-	peritoneum
20. degluti/o-	swallowing	49. periton/o-	peritoneum
21. digest/o-	break down food; digest	50. pharyng/o-	pharynx (throat)
22. duoden/o-	duodenum (first part of small intestine)	51. proct/o-	rectum and anus
23. emulsific/o-	droplets of fat suspended in a liquid	52. pylor/o-	pylorus
24. enter/o-	intestine	53. rect/o-	rectum
25. esophag/o-	esophagus	54. saliv/o-	saliva
26. fec/a-	feces; stool	55. sial/o-	saliva; salivary gland
27. fec/o-	feces; stool	56. sigmoid/o-	sigmoid colon
28. gastr/o-	stomach	57. stal/o-	contraction
29. gloss/o-	tongue	58. stomat/o-	mouth

Combining Form and Suffix Exercise

Read the definition of the medical word. Look at the combining form that is given. Select the correct suffix from the Suffix List and write it on the blank line. Then build the medical word and write it on the line. (Remember: You may need to remove the combining vowel. Always remove the hyphens and slash.) Be sure to check your spelling. The first one has been done for you.

SUFFIX LIST			
-ac (pertaining to)	-ation (a process; being or having)	-gen (that which produces)	-ion (action; condition)
-al (pertaining to)	-cyte (cell)	-ic (pertaining to)	-ive (pertaining to)
-ary (pertaining to)	-eal (pertaining to)	-in (a substance)	-ory (having the function of)
-ase (enzyme)			

Definition of the Medical Word	Combining Form	Suffix	Build the Medical Word
1. Pertaining to the intestine	intestin/o-	-al	intestinal

(You think *pertaining to* (-al) + *the intestine* (intestin/o-). You change the order of the word parts to put the suffix last. You write *intestinal*.)

2. Pertaining to the stomach	gastr/o-	-ic	gastric
3. Liver cell	hepat/o-	-cyte	hepatocyte
4. Pertaining to the mouth	or/o-	-al	oral
5. Pertaining to (a gland that makes) saliva	saliv/o-	-ary	salivary
6. Action that breaks down or digests food	digest/o-	-ion	digestion
7. Process of chewing	mastic/o-	-ation	mastication
8. Pertaining to the rectum	rect/o-	-al	rectal
9. Enzyme (that digests) fat	lip/o-	-ase	lipase
10. Pertaining to the appendix	appendic/o-	-eal	appendiceal
11. Pertaining to food and nourishment	aliment/o-	-ary	alimentary
12. Pertaining to the colon	colon/o-	-ic	colonic
13. Pertaining to digestion	digest/o-	-ive	digestive
14. Pertaining to the esophagus	esophag/o-	-eal	esophageal
15. That which produces pepsin	pepsin/o-	-gen	pepsinogen
16. Pertaining to the pancreas	pancreat/o-	-ic	pancreatic
17. Pertaining to bile	bil/i-	-ary	biliary
18. Pertaining to the duodenum	duoden/o-	-al	duodenal
19. Having the function of the sense of taste	gustat/o-	-ory	gustatory
20. Pertaining to the throat	pharyng/o-	-eal	pharyngeal
21. A substance (produced by the) stomach	gastr/o-	-in	gastrin
22. Pertaining to the pylorus	pylor/o-	-ic	pyloric
23. Pertaining to the jejunum	jejun/o-	-al	jejun/o-
24. Pertaining to the abdomen	celi/o-	-ac	celiac
25. Pertaining to feces	fec/o-	-al	fecal
26. Action (in which something is) absorbed	absorpt/o-	-ion	absorption
27. Enzyme (that digests) milk	lact/o-	-ase	lactase
28. A process of having fat droplets suspended in a liquid	emulsific/o-	-ation	emulsification
29. Pertaining to the peritoneum	peritone/o-	-al	peritoneal

Prefix Exercise

Read the definition of the medical word. Look at the medical word or partial word that is given (it already contains a combining form and a suffix). Select the correct prefix from the Prefix List and write it on the blank line. Then build the medical word and write it on the line. Be sure to check your spelling. The first one has been done for you.

PREFIX LIST			
de- (reversal of; without)	meso- (middle)	peri- (around)	sub- (below; underneath; less than)

Definition of the Medical Word	Prefix	Word or Partial Word	Build the Medical Word
1. Pertaining to (the salivary gland that is) underneath the mandible	sub-	mandibular	submandibular
2. Process around (the intestine of) contraction	peri-	stalsis	peristalsis
3. Pertaining to the middle of the intestine *Hint: Delete the o on the prefix before building this word.*	meso-	enteric	mesenteric
4. A process (of being) without stool	de-	fecation	defecation
5. Pertaining to (being) underneath the tongue	sub-	lingual	sublingual

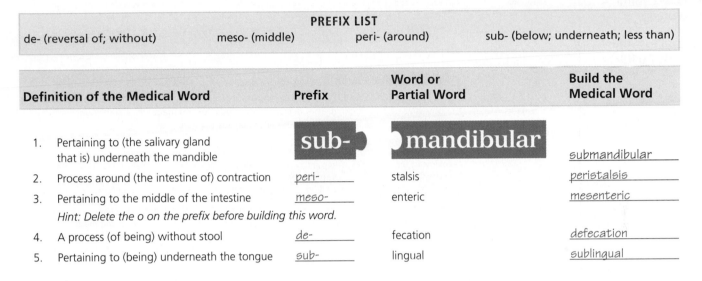

Multiple Combining Forms and Suffix Exercise

Read the definition of the medical word. Select the correct suffix and combining forms. Then build the medical word and write it on the line. Be sure to check your spelling. The first one has been done for you.

SUFFIX LIST	COMBINING FORM LIST		
-al (pertaining to) -ic (pertaining to) -in (a substance) -logy (the study of)	abdomin/o- (abdomen) chlor/o- (chloride) cholecyst/o- (gallbladder)	enter/o- (intestine) gastr/o- (stomach) hydr/o- (water; fluid)	intestin/o- (intestine) kin/o- (movement) pelv/o- (pelvis)

Definition of the Medical Word	Combining Form	Combining Form	Suffix	Build the Medical Word
1. Pertaining to (an acid made of) water and chloride	hydr/o-	chlor/o-	-ic	hydrochloric

(You think *pertaining to* (-ic) + *water* (hydr/o-) + *chloride* (chlor/o-). You change the order of the word parts to put the suffix last. You write *hydrochloric*.)

Definition of the Medical Word	Combining Form	Combining Form	Suffix	Build the Medical Word
2. Pertaining to the stomach and intestine	gastr/o-	intestin/o-	-al	gastrointestinal
3. Pertaining to the abdomen and pelvis	abdomin/o-	pelv/o-	-ic	abdominopelvic
4. The study of the stomach and intestines	gastr/o-	enter/o-	-logy	gastroenterology
5. A substance (that causes the) gallbladder to move (and contract)	cholecyst/o-	kin/o-	-in	cholecystokinin

ETYMOLOGY

odynophagia
(oh-DIN-oh-FAY-jee-ah)

　odyn/o-　*pain*

　phag/o-　*eating; swallowing*

MEDIA RESOURCES

See the PowerPoint presentation on www.myhealthprofessionskit.com for videos on the following topics covered in this chapter:

- Anorexia
- Bulimia

Diseases and Conditions

Eating

Word or Phrase	Description	Word Building
anorexia	Decreased appetite because of disease or the gastrointestinal side effects of a drug. The patient is said to be **anorexic**. Treatment: Correct the underlying cause.	**anorexia** (AN-oh-REK-see-ah) 　**an-** *without; not* 　**orex/o-** *appetite* 　**-ia** *condition; state; thing* **anorexic** (AN-oh-REK-sik)

Clinical Connections

Psychiatry (Chapter 17). Anorexia nervosa is a psychiatric disorder in which patients have an obsessive desire to be thin. They decrease their food intake to the point of starvation, not because they have no appetite, but because they see themselves as being fat.

Word or Phrase	Description	Word Building
dysphagia	Difficult or painful eating or swallowing. A stroke can make it difficult to coordinate the muscles for eating and swallowing. An oral infection or poorly fitted dentures can cause painful eating. Treatment: Soft foods and thickened liquids. Antibiotic drugs for an oral bacterial infection.	**dysphagia** (dis-FAY-jee-ah) 　**dys-** *painful; difficult; abnormal* 　**phag/o-** *eating; swallowing* 　**-ia** *condition; state; thing*
polyphagia	Excessive overeating due to an overactive thyroid gland, diabetes mellitus, or a psychiatric illness. Treatment: Correct the underlying cause.	**polyphagia** (PAWL-ee-FAY-jee-ah) 　**poly-** *many; much* 　**phag/o-** *eating; swallowing* 　**-ia** *condition; state; thing*

Mouth and Lips

Word or Phrase	Description	Word Building
cheilitis	Inflammation and cracking of the lips and corners of the mouth due to infection, allergies, or nutritional deficiency. Treatment: Correct the underlying cause.	**cheilitis** (ky-LY-tis) 　**cheil/o-** *lip* 　**-itis** *inflammation of; infection of*
sialolithiasis	A stone (**sialolith**) that forms in the salivary gland and becomes lodged in the duct, blocking the flow of saliva. The salivary gland, mouth, and face become swollen. When the salivary gland contracts, the duct spasms, causing pain. Treatment: Surgical removal of the stone.	**sialolithiasis** (sy-AL-oh-lih-THY-ah-sis) 　**sial/o-** *saliva; salivary gland* 　**lith/o-** *stone* 　**-iasis** *state of; process of* **sialolith** (sy-AL-oh-lith) 　**sial/o-** *saliva; salivary gland* 　**-lith** *stone*

Activity

Sound-Alike Words

Dysphagia (difficult or painful eating) can be confused with dysphasia (difficult speech). Use this memory aid to help you remember the difference: dysphagia has to do with eating and it has the letters GI (gastrointestinal) in it.

Word or Phrase	Description	Word Building
stomatitis	Inflammation of the oral mucosa. Stomatitis can be caused by poorly fitting dentures or infection. **Aphthous stomatitis** consists of small ulcers (canker sores) of the oral mucosa. Its cause is unknown. **Glossitis** is an inflammation that involves only the tongue (see Figure 3-8 ■). Treatment: Correct the underlying cause.	**stomatitis** (STOH-mah-TY-tis) 　**stomat/o-** mouth 　**-itis** inflammation of; infection of **aphthous** (AF-thus) 　**aphth/o-** ulcer 　**-ous** pertaining to **glossitis** (glaw-SY-tis) 　**gloss/o-** tongue 　**-itis** inflammation of; infection of

Figure 3-8 ■ Glossitis.
This inflammation of the tongue was caused by a viral infection. Other causes of glossitis include bacterial infection, food allergy, abrasive or spicy foods, or a vitamin B deficiency.

Esophagus and Stomach

Word or Phrase	Description	Word Building
dyspepsia	**Indigestion** or epigastric pain that may be accompanied by gas or nausea. It can be caused by excess stomach acid or reflux of stomach acid into the esophagus, overeating, spicy foods, or stress. Treatment: Antacid drugs. Avoid things that cause it.	**dyspepsia** (dis-PEP-see-ah) 　**dys-** painful; difficult; abnormal 　**peps/o-** digestion 　**-ia** condition; state; thing
esophageal varices	Swollen, protruding veins in the mucosa of the lower esophagus or stomach (see Figure 3-9 ■). When liver disease causes blood to back up in the large vein from the intestines to the liver, the blood is forced to take an alternate route through the gastroesophageal veins, but eventually these veins become engorged. Esophageal and gastric varices are easily irritated by passing food. They can hemorrhage suddenly, causing death. Treatment: Correct the underlying liver disease. Surgery: A drug is injected into the varix to harden it and block the blood flow.	**varix** (VAIR-iks) **varices** (VAIR-ih-seez) *Varix* is a Latin singular noun. Form the plural by changing *-ix* to *-ices.*

Figure 3-9 ■ Esophageal varix.
A varix is a dilated, swollen vein in the mucosa. This esophageal varix was seen through an endoscope passed through the mouth and into the esophagus. There are dark areas of old blood from previous bleeding.

ETYMOLOGY

indigestion
(IN-dy-JES-chun)

　in-　in; within; not

　digest/o-　break down food; digest

　-ion　action; condition

See the PowerPoint
presentation on
www.myhealthprofes
sionskit.com for videos
on the following topics
covered in this chapter:

- Eating disorders
- GERD

ETYMOLOGY

Reflux comes from a
Latin word meaning *a
backward flow.*

Emesis is a Greek word
and vomitus is a Latin
word meaning *ejected
contents.*

Word or Phrase	Description	Word Building
gastritis	Acute or chronic inflammation of the stomach due to spicy foods, excess acid production, or a bacterial infection. Treatment: Antacid drugs, antibiotic drugs for a bacterial infection.	**gastritis** (gas-TRY-tis) **gastr/o-** *stomach* **-itis** *inflammation of; infection of*
gastroenteritis	Acute inflammation or infection of the stomach and intestines due to a virus (flu) or bacterium (contaminated food). There is abdominal pain, nausea, vomiting, and diarrhea. Treatment: Antiemetic drugs (to prevent vomiting), antidiarrheal drugs, antibiotic drugs for a bacterial infection.	**gastroenteritis** (GAS-troh-EN-ter-EYE-tis) **gastr/o-** *stomach* **enter/o-** *intestine* **-itis** *inflammation of; infection of*
gastroesophageal reflux disease (GERD)	Chronic inflammation and irritation due to **reflux** of stomach acid back into the esophagus. This occurs because the lower esophageal sphincter does not close tightly. There is a sore throat, belching, and **esophagitis** with chronic inflammation. This can lead to esophageal ulcers or cancer of the esophagus. Treatment: Eat small, frequent meals, not large meals. Elevate the head of the bed while sleeping. Avoid alcohol and foods that stimulate acid secretion. Treatment: Antacid drugs to neutralize acid, drugs that decrease the production of acid.	**gastroesophageal** (GAS-troh-ee-SAWF-ah-JEE-al) **gastr/o-** *stomach* **esophag/o-** *esophagus* **-eal** *pertaining to* **reflux** (REE-fluks) **esophagitis** (ee-SAWF-ah-JY-tis) **esophag/o-** *esophagus* **-itis** *inflammation of; infection of*
heartburn	Temporary inflammation of the esophagus due to reflux of stomach acid. It is also known as **pyrosis**. Treatment: Antacid drugs.	**pyrosis** (py-ROH-sis) **pyr/o-** *fire; burning* **-osis** *condition; abnormal condition; process*
hematemesis	Vomiting of blood (emesis) because of bleeding in the stomach or esophagus. This can be due to an esophageal or gastric ulcer or esophageal varices. Coffee-grounds emesis contains old, dark blood that has been partially digested by the stomach. Treatment: Correct the underlying cause.	**hematemesis** (HEE-mah-TEM-eh-sis) **hemat/o-** *blood* **-emesis** *vomiting*
nausea and vomiting (N&V)	Nausea is an unpleasant, queasy feeling in the stomach that precedes the urge to vomit. The patient is said to be nauseated. It is caused by inflammation or infection of the stomach or by motion sickness. Vomiting or **emesis** is the expelling of food from the stomach through the mouth. It is triggered when impulses from the stomach or inner ear stimulate the vomiting center in the brain. Vomit or **vomitus** is the expelled food or chyme. Projectile vomiting is vomitus expelled with force and projected a distance from the patient. Retching (dry heaves) is continual vomiting when there is no longer anything in the stomach. **Regurgitation** is the reflux of small amounts of food and acid back into the mouth, but without vomiting. Treatment: Antiemetic drugs.	**nausea** (NAW-see-ah) (NAW-zha) **emesis** (EM-eh-sis) **vomitus** (VAWM-ih-tus) **regurgitation** (ree-GER-jih-TAY-shun) **regurgitat/o-** *flow backward* **-ion** *action; condition*

Clinical Connections

Obstetrics (Chapter 13). **Hyperemesis gravidarum** is excessive vomiting during the first months of pregnancy. It is thought to be due to changes in hormone levels that occur during pregnancy.	**hyperemesis** (HY-per-EM-eh-sis) **hyper-** *above; more than normal* **-emesis** *condition of vomiting* **gravidarum** (GRAV-ih-DAIR-um) *Gravidarum* means *of pregnancy.*

Talking Point

Heartburn

Chocolate, peppermint, coffee, carbonated beverages, alcoholic beverages, fatty foods and fried foods, citrus fruits and juices, pepper, vinegar, ketchup, and mustard are the foods most likely to cause heartburn.

Source: American Gastroenterological Association.

Activity

Regurgitation

From a novelty store, get a pile of rubber vomit. This can be brought out when the medical word "regurgitate" is discussed, but it can also be used to make the additional point that students should not just regurgitate facts back to the instructor. They should really seek to understand what they are learning!

Word or Phrase	Description	Word Building

peptic ulcer disease (PUD)	Chronic irritation, burning pain, and erosion of the mucosa to form an ulcer. An esophageal ulcer, a gastric ulcer in the stomach, and a duodenal ulcer are all peptic ulcers. Gastric ulcers are most commonly caused by the bacterium *Helicobacter pylori* (see Figure 3-10 ■). Ulcers can also be caused by excessive hydrochloric acid, stress, and by drugs (such as aspirin) that irritate the mucosa. Treatment: Antibiotic drugs to treat *H. pylori* infection. Drugs to decrease acid production. Antacid drugs. Avoid spicy foods, smoking, alcohol, caffeine, and aspirin-containing drugs.	**peptic** (PEP-tik)
		    pept/o- *digestion*
		    -ic *pertaining to*
		ulcer (UL-ser)

Figure 3-10 ■ Gastric ulcer.
This gastric mucosa is raw and irritated with a large central ulcer crater. The dark blood clot indicates a recent episode of bleeding from the ulcer.

Word or Phrase	Description	Word Building

stomach cancer	**Cancerous** tumor of the stomach that usually begins in glands in the gastric mucosa. It is also known as gastric **adenocarcinoma.** It can develop due to chronic irritation from a *Helicobacter pylori* infection. Treatment: Surgery to remove the cancerous tumor and part of the stomach (gastrectomy).	**cancerous** (KAN-ser-us)
		    cancer/o- *cancer*
		    -ous *pertaining to*
		adenocarcinoma (AD-eh-noh-KAR-sih-NOH-mah)
		    aden/o- *gland*
		    carcin/o- *cancer*
		    -oma *tumor; mass*

Duodenum, Jejunum, Ileum

Word or Phrase	Description	Word Building

ileus	Abnormal absence of peristalsis in the small and large intestines. Obstipation, a tumor, adhesions, or a hernia can cause a mechanical obstruction. A severe infection in the intestine or abdominopelvic cavity, trauma, shock, or drugs can cause a paralytic ileus. **Postoperative ileus** occurs after the intestines are manipulated during abdominal surgery and peristalsis is slow to return. Treatment: Intravenous fluids for temporary nutritional support. Surgery (bowel resection and anastomosis) may be needed.	**ileus** (IL-ee-us)
		postoperative (post-AWP-er-ah-tiv)
		    post- *after; behind*
		    operat/o- *perform a procedure; surgery*
		    -ive *pertaining to*

ETYMOLOGY

Ulcer comes from a Latin word meaning *a sore.*

ETYMOLOGY

Cancer is a Latin word meaning *a crab.* Cancer spreads in all directions like the legs of a crab spread out from its body.

ETYMOLOGY

Ileus is a Latin word meaning *rolled up and tightly obstructed.*

Activity

Check It Out

Have students look in their medicine cabinets at home and name all of the prescription and over-the-counter drugs that are used to treat symptoms of the GI tract. Tell them to be sure to spell the drug name correctly.

Have students go to the American Gastroenterological Association website (www.gastro.org). Tell them to click on the public section, then click the digestive health resource center, and then choose a gastrointestinal disease site. Have them write a brief one-page summary of the information about that disease.

Word or Phrase	Description	Word Building
intussusception	Telescoping of one segment of intestine inside the lumen of the next segment (see Figure 3-11a ■). There is vomiting and abdominal pain. The cause is unknown. Treatment: Surgery (bowel resection and anastomosis).	**intussusception** (IN-tus-suh-SEP-shun) **intussuscep/o-** *to receive within* **-tion** *a process; being or having*

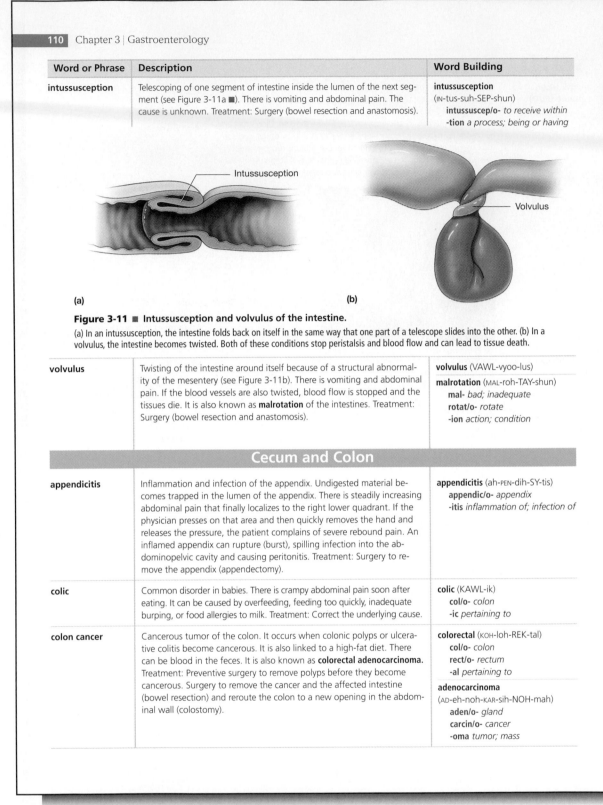

Figure 3-11 ■ Intussusception and volvulus of the intestine.
(a) In an intussusception, the intestine folds back on itself in the same way that one part of a telescope slides into the other. (b) In a volvulus, the intestine becomes twisted. Both of these conditions stop peristalsis and blood flow and can lead to tissue death.

Word or Phrase	Description	Word Building
volvulus	Twisting of the intestine around itself because of a structural abnormality of the mesentery (see Figure 3-11b). There is vomiting and abdominal pain. If the blood vessels are also twisted, blood flow is stopped and the tissues die. It is also known as **malrotation** of the intestines. Treatment: Surgery (bowel resection and anastomosis).	**volvulus** (VAWL-vyoo-lus) **malrotation** (MAL-roh-TAY-shun) **mal-** *bad; inadequate* **rotat/o-** *rotate* **-ion** *action; condition*

Cecum and Colon

Word or Phrase	Description	Word Building
appendicitis	Inflammation and infection of the appendix. Undigested material becomes trapped in the lumen of the appendix. There is steadily increasing abdominal pain that finally localizes to the right lower quadrant. If the physician presses on that area and then quickly removes the hand and releases the pressure, the patient complains of severe rebound pain. An inflamed appendix can rupture (burst), spilling infection into the abdominopelvic cavity and causing peritonitis. Treatment: Surgery to remove the appendix (appendectomy).	**appendicitis** (ah-PEN-dih-SY-tis) **appendic/o-** *appendix* **-itis** *inflammation of; infection of*
colic	Common disorder in babies. There is crampy abdominal pain soon after eating. It can be caused by overfeeding, feeding too quickly, inadequate burping, or food allergies to milk. Treatment: Correct the underlying cause.	**colic** (KAWL-ik) **col/o-** *colon* **-ic** *pertaining to*
colon cancer	Cancerous tumor of the colon. It occurs when colonic polyps or ulcerative colitis become cancerous. It is also linked to a high-fat diet. There can be blood in the feces. It is also known as **colorectal adenocarcinoma.** Treatment: Preventive surgery to remove polyps before they become cancerous. Surgery to remove the cancer and the affected intestine (bowel resection) and reroute the colon to a new opening in the abdominal wall (colostomy).	**colorectal** (KOH-loh-REK-tal) **col/o-** *colon* **rect/o-** *rectum* **-al** *pertaining to* **adenocarcinoma** (AD-eh-noh-KAR-sih-NOH-mah) **aden/o-** *gland* **carcin/o-** *cancer* **-oma** *tumor; mass*

MEDIA RESOURCES

See the PowerPoint presentation on www.myhealthprofessionskit.com for an animation on appendicitis.

Activity

Word Study

Have students use an English and a medical dictionary to answer a question about the etymology of this word.

Why did appendicitis used to be called "typhilitis" in the 1800s?

Word or Phrase	Description	Word Building

diverticulum	Weakness in the wall of the colon where the mucosa forms a pouch or tube. Diverticula can be caused by eating a low fiber diet that forms small, compact feces. Then, increased intra-abdominal pressure and straining to pass those feces eventually creates diverticula. **Diverticulosis** or diverticular disease is the condition of multiple diverticula (see Figure 3-12 ■). If feces become trapped inside a diverticulum, this causes inflammation, infection, abdominal pain, and fever, a condition known as **diverticulitis** (see Figure 3-13 ■). Prevention: High-fiber diet. Treatment: Antibiotic drugs to treat diverticulitis. Surgery (bowel resection and anastomosis) to remove the affected segment of intestine.	**diverticulum** (DY-ver-TIK-yoo lum)
		
		diverticula (DY-ver-TIK-yoo-lah)
		Diverticulum is a Latin singular noun. Form the plural by changing *-um* to *-a*.
		
		diverticulosis
		(DY-ver-TIK-yoo-LOH-sis)
		  diverticul/o- *diverticulum*
		  -osis *condition; abnormal condition; process*
		
		diverticulitis
		(DY-ver-TIK-yoo-LY-tis)
		  diverticul/o- *diverticulum*
		  -itis *inflammation of; infection of*

Figure 3-12 ■ Diverticula.
These openings in the wall of the colon lead to diverticular sacs where feces can become trapped.

Pedunculated polyp
Stalk of polyp
Sessile polyp
Diverticulum with diverticulitis
Haustra
Mucosal folds

Figure 3-13 ■ Diverticulitis and polyposis.
This diverticulum has become infected from trapped feces. These polyps are irritated by the passage of feces and can become cancerous.

Clinical Connections

Dietetics. Diverticular disease was unknown until the early 1900s, when refined flour began to replace whole wheat flour. Diverticular disease is common in countries where people eat a low-fiber diet, but is uncommon in third-world countries where there is a high-fiber diet. Fiber creates bulk and holds water to keep the feces soft.

Word or Phrase	Description	Word Building

dysentery	Bacterial infection caused by an unusual strain of *E. coli*, a common bacterium in the large intestine. There is watery diarrhea mixed with blood and mucus. Treatment: Antibiotic drugs.	**dysentery** (DIS-en-TAIR-ee)
		  dys- *painful; difficult; abnormal*
		  -entery *condition of the intestine*
		The ending *-entery* contains the combining form *enter/o-* and the one-letter suffix *-y*.

Word or Phrase	Description	Word Building

gluten enteropathy	A food allergy and toxic reaction to the gluten found in certain grains (wheat, barley, rye, oats). The small intestine is damaged by the allergic response. It is also known as **celiac disease.** Treatment: Avoid eating foods and food products that contain gluten.	**gluten** (GLOO-ten)
		
		enteropathy (EN-ter-AWP-ah-thee)
		    enter/o- *intestine*
		    -pathy *disease; suffering*
		
		celiac (SEE-lee-ak)
		    celi/o- *abdomen*
		    -ac *pertaining to*

inflammatory bowel disease (IBD)	Chronic inflammation of various parts of the small and large intestines. There is diarrhea, bloody feces, abdominal cramps, and fever. The cause is not known. There are two types of inflammatory bowel disease: (1) **Crohn's disease** or **regional enteritis** affects the ileum and colon (see Figure 3-14 ■). There are areas of normal mucosa ("skip areas") and then inflammation. There are ulcers and thickening of the intestinal wall that can cause a partial obstruction in the intestine. (2) **Ulcerative colitis** affects the colon and rectum and causes inflammation and ulcers. Treatment: Corticosteroid drugs to decrease inflammation. Surgery (bowel resection) to remove the affected area and reroute the intestine to a new opening in the abdominal wall (ileostomy, colostomy).	**Crohn** (KROHN)
		
		enteritis (EN-ter-EYE-tis)
		    enter/o- *intestine*
		    -itis *inflammation of; infection of*
		
		ulcerative (UL-sir-ah-tiv)
		    ulcerat/o- *ulcer*
		    -ive *pertaining to*
		
		colitis (koh-LY-tis)
		    col/o- *colon*
		    -itis *inflammation of; infection of*

Cobblestone appearance

Area dilated due to obstruction

Partial obstruction of the ileum

Thickening of wall of ileum

Ulcers

Skip area

(a)   (b)

Figure 3-14 ■ Crohn's disease.

(a) This x-ray shows the characteristic cobblestone appearance of Crohn's disease. (b) It is due to thickening of the intestinal wall and ulcers. There is also a partial obstruction.

irritable bowel syndrome (IBS)	Disorder of the function of the colon, although the mucosa of the colon never shows any visible signs of inflammation. A syndrome consists of interrelated symptoms and signs. There is cramping, abdominal pain, diarrhea, bloating alternating with constipation, and excessive mucus. The cause is not known but may be related to lactose intolerance and emotional stress. It is also known as **spastic colon** or **mucous colitis.** Treatment: Antidiarrheal, antispasmodic, and antianxiety drugs. High-fiber diet and laxative drugs to prevent constipation.	**spastic** (SPAS-tik)
		    spast/o- *spasm*
		    -ic *pertaining to*
		
		colitis (koh-LY-tis)
		    col/o- *colon*
		    -itis *inflammation of; infection of*

ETYMOLOGY

Peduncle comes from a Latin word meaning *a stalk with a little foot.*

Sessile comes from a Latin word meaning *low growing with a broad base.*

Benign comes from a Latin word meaning *kind, not harmful.*

Word or Phrase	Description	Word Building
polyp	Small, fleshy, benign or precancerous growth in the mucosa of the colon. A **pedunculated polyp** has a thin stalk that supports an irregular, ball-shaped top (see Figure 3-13). A **sessile polyp** is a mound with a broad base (see Figure 3-15 ■). **Benign familial polyposis** is an inherited condition in which family members have multiple colon polyps. Although all polyps initially are benign, they can become cancerous. Treatment: Surgery to remove the polyps (polypectomy).	**polyp** (PAW-lip) **pedunculated** (peh-DUNG-kyoo-lay-ted) **sessile** (SES-il) **benign** (bee-NINE) **polyposis** (PAWL-ee-POH-sis) polyp/o- *polyp* -osis *condition; abnormal condition; process*

Figure 3-15 ■ Colonic polyps.
This patient has multiple sessile polyps protruding through the many haustra (folds) in the wall of the colon.

Rectum and Anus

hemorrhoids	Swollen, protruding veins in the rectum (internal hemorrhoids) or on the skin around the anus (external hemorrhoids). They are caused by increased intra-abdominal pressure from straining during a bowel movement. This dilates the veins with blood until they permanently protrude. They are also known as **piles.** A hemorrhoid is irritated as feces go by it, and its surface bleeds easily. Treatment: Topical corticosteroid drugs to decrease itching and irritation. Surgery to remove the hemorrhoids (hemorrhoidectomy).	**hemorrhoid** (HEM-oh-royd) hemorrh/o- *a flowing of blood* -oid *resembling*
proctitis	Inflammation of the rectum due to radiation therapy or ulcers or infection of the rectum	**proctitis** (prawk-TY-tis) proct/o- *rectum* -itis *inflammation of; infection of*
rectocele	Protruding wall of the rectum pushes on the adjacent vaginal wall, causing it to collapse inward and block the vaginal canal. Treatment: Surgery to repair the defect.	**rectocele** (REK-toh-seel) rect/o- *rectum* -cele *hernia*

Defecation and Feces

constipation	Failure to have regular, soft bowel movements. This can be due to decreased peristalsis, lack of dietary fiber, inadequate water intake, or the side effect of a drug. **Obstipation** is severe, unrelieved constipation that can lead to a mechanical obstruction of the bowel. The patient is said to be obstipated. A **fecalith** is hardened feces that becomes a stonelike mass. This can form in the appendix or in a diverticulum. It can be seen when an abdominal x-ray is done. Treatment: Laxative drugs, a high-fiber diet, increased water intake, enemas.	**constipation** (CON-stih-PAY-shun) constip/o- *compacted feces* -ation *a process; being or having* **obstipation** (AWB-stih-PAY-shun) obstip/o- *severe constipation* -ation *a process; being or having* **fecalith** (FEE-kah-lith) fec/a- *feces; stool* -lith *stone*

Word or Phrase	Description	Word Building
diarrhea	Abnormally frequent, loose, and sometimes watery feces. It is caused by an infection (bacteria, viruses), irritable bowel syndrome, ulcerative colitis, lactose intolerance, or the side effect of a drug. There is increased peristalsis, and the feces move through the large intestine before the water can be absorbed. Treatment: Antidiarrheal drugs, lactase supplements. Antibiotic drugs to treat bacterial infections.	**diarrhea** (DY-ah-REE-ah) **dia-** *complete; completely through* **-rrhea** *flow; discharge* The ending *-rrhea* contains the combining form *rrhe/o-* and the one-letter suffix *-a*.
flatulence	Presence of excessive amounts of flatus (gas) in the stomach or intestines. It can be caused by milk (lactose intolerance), indigestion, or incomplete digestion of carbohydrates such as beans. Treatment: Lactase supplements, antigas drugs.	**flatulence** (FLAT-yoo-lens) **flatul/o-** *flatus (gas)* **-ence** *state of*
hematochezia	Blood in the feces. The source of bleeding can be an ulcer, cancer, Crohn's disease, polyp, diverticulum, or hemorrhoid. Bright red blood indicates active bleeding in the lower gastrointestinal system. **Melena** is a dark, tar-like feces that contains digested blood from bleeding in the esophagus or stomach. Treatment: Correct the underlying cause of bleeding.	**hematochezia** (hee-MAH-toh-KEE-zee-ah) **hemat/o-** *blood* **chez/o-** *to pass feces* **-ia** *condition; state; thing* **melena** (meh-LEE-nah)
incontinence	Inability to voluntarily control bowel movements. A patient with paralysis of the lower extremities lacks sensation and motor control of the external anal sphincter and is incontinent. Patients with dementia are unaware of a bowel movement. Treatment: None.	**incontinence** (in-CON-tih-nens) **in-** *in; within, not* **contin/o-** *hold together* **-ence** *state of* Select the correct prefix meaning to get the definition of *incontinence*: *a state of not holding together (feces).*
steatorrhea	Greasy, frothy, foul-smelling feces that contain undigested fats. There is not enough of the enzyme lipase because of pancreatic disease or cystic fibrosis. Treatment: Correct the underlying cause.	**steatorrhea** (stee-AT-oh-REE-ah) **steat/o-** *fat* **-rrhea** *flow; discharge*

ETYMOLOGY

Melena comes from a Greek word meaning *black*.

Across the Life Span

Pediatrics. Feces forms in the intestine while the fetus is in the uterus. Swallowed amniotic fluid and sloughed-off fetal skin cells mix with mucus and bile to form **meconium,** a thick, sticky, green-to-black waste that is passed after birth. In the newborn nursery, the nurse checks to see that the anus and rectum are **patent** (open). Occasionally, a newborn will have an **imperforate anus.** This is a congenital (present at birth) abnormality in which there is no anal opening. Treatment: Immediate surgery to open the anus and connect the rectum to the outside of the body.

meconium (meh-KOH-nee-um)

patent (PAY-tent)

imperforate anus (im-PER-for-ate) **im-** *not* **perfor/o-** *to have an opening* **-ate** *composed of; pertaining to*

Geriatrics. Constipation is a common complaint in older adults. A diet of refined foods with low fiber, lack of water intake, and inactivity contribute to the formation of small, hard feces. Narcotic drugs used to treat chronic pain cause constipation and can actually cause a bowel obstruction in older adults. Some older patients are incontinent of feces (unable to voluntarily control their bowel movements). This can be due to a decrease in the size of the rectum because of a rectocele, impairment of anal sphincter function because of nerve damage, or mental impairment and dementia in which the patient is unaware that a bowel movement is occurring.

Abdominal Wall and Abdominal Cavity

Word or Phrase	Description	Word Building

adhesions	Fibrous bands that form after abdominal surgery. They bind the intestines to each other or to other organs. They can bind so tightly that peristalsis and intestinal function are affected. Treatment: Surgery to cut the fibrous adhesions (lysis of adhesions).	**adhesion** (ad-HEE-zhun)
		  adhes/o- *to stick to*
		  -ion *action; condition*

hernia	Weakness in the muscle of the diaphragm or abdominal wall. The intestine bulges through the defect. There is swelling and pain. There is an inherited tendency to hernias, but hernias can also be caused by pregnancy, obesity, or heavy lifting. Treatment: Surgery to correct the hernia (herniorrhaphy).
	
	1. Hernias are named according to how easily the intestines can move back into their normal position. A sliding or reducible hernia moves back and forth between the hernia sac and the abdominopelvic cavity (see Figure 3-16a ■). In an **incarcerated (irreducible) hernia,** the intestine swells in the hernia sac and becomes trapped. The intestine can no longer be pushed back into the abdomen. A **strangulated hernia** is an incarcerated hernia whose blood supply has been cut off (see Figure 3-16b). This leads to tissue death (necrosis).
	2. Hernias are named according to their location. With a **hiatal hernia,** the stomach bulges through the normal opening in the diaphragm for the esophagus. A **ventral hernia** is anywhere on the anterior abdominal wall (except at the umbilicus). An **umbilical hernia** is at the umbilicus (navel). An **omphalocele** is an umbilical hernia that is present at birth and is only covered with peritoneum, without any fat or abdominal skin (see Figure 3-16c). An **inguinal hernia** is in the groin. In a male patient with an inguinal hernia, the intestine slides through the inguinal canal and into the scrotum. An **incisional hernia** is along the suture line of a prior abdominal surgical incision.
		hernia (HER-nee-ah)
		
		incarcerated (in-KAR-seh-ray-ted)
		  incarcer/o- *to imprison*
		  -ated *pertaining to a condition; composed of*
		
		hiatal (hy-AA-tal)
		  hiat/o- *gap; opening*
		  -al *pertaining to*
		
		ventral (VEN-tral)
		  ventr/o- *front; abdomen*
		  -al *pertaining to*
		
		umbilical (um-BIL-ih-kal)
		  umbilic/o- *umbilicus; navel*
		  -al *pertaining to*
		
		omphalocele (OM-fal-oh-seel)
		  omphal/o- *umbilicus; navel*
		  -cele *hernia*
		
		inguinal (ING-gwih-nal)
		  inguin/o- *groin*
		  -al *pertaining to*
		
		incisional (in-SIH-shun-al)
		  incis/o- *to cut into*
		  -ion *action; condition*
		  -al *pertaining to*

ETYMOLOGY

Hernia is a Latin word meaning *a rupture*.

Hiatal is a Latin word meaning *an opening*.

SLIDING HERNIA
Loop of intestine in hernia sac

(a)

STRANGULATED HERNIA
Entrapped, necrotic loop of intestine

(b)

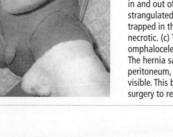

(c)

Figure 3-16 ■ Hernia.

(a) In a sliding hernia, the intestine moves in and out of the hernia sac. (b) In a strangulated hernia, the intestine is trapped in the hernia sac and becomes necrotic. (c) This baby was born with an omphalocele, a hernia at the umbilicus. The hernia sac is only a layer of peritoneum, and the intestine inside is visible. This baby will have immediate surgery to repair the hernia.

Word or Phrase	Description	Word Building
peritonitis	Inflammation and infection of the peritoneum (see Figure 3-17 ■). It occurs when an ulcer, diverticulum, or cancerous tumor eats through the wall of the stomach or intestines or when an inflamed appendix ruptures. Drainage and bacteria spill into the abdominopelvic cavity. Treatment: Surgery (exploratory laparotomy) to clean out the abdominal cavity. Correct the underlying cause. Antibiotic drugs for bacterial infection.	**peritonitis** (PAIR-ih-toh-NY-tis) **periton/o-** *peritoneum* **-itis** *inflammation of; infection of*

Figure 3-17 ■ **Peritonitis.**
This patient developed peritonitis when a duodendal ulcer perforated the intestinal wall and spilled green bile and chyme into the abdominal cavity. The areas of white are large numbers of white blood cells (pus) that are fighting this infection.

Liver

Word or Phrase	Description	Word Building
ascites	Accumulation of **ascitic** fluid in the abdominopelvic cavity. Liver disease and congestive heart failure cause a backup of blood. This increases the blood pressure in the veins of the abdomen. This pressure pushes fluid out of the blood and into the abdominopelvic cavity. Treatment: Removal of ascitic fluid from the abdomen using a needle (abdominocentesis). Surgery: Permanent drainage of excess fluid via an implanted tube (shunt).	**ascites** (ah-SY-teez) **ascitic** (ah-SIT-ik) **ascit/o-** *ascites* **-ic** *pertaining to*

Word Alert

SOUND-ALIKE WORDS

acidic   (adjective)   Pertaining to an acid, having a low pH
Example: Hydrochloric acid creates an acidic (low pH) environment in the stomach.

ascitic   (adjective)   Pertaining to ascites
Example: Ascitic fluid accumulates and causes the abdominal wall to bulge outward.

Word or Phrase	Description	Word Building
cirrhosis	Chronic, progressive inflammation and finally irreversible degeneration of the liver, with nodules and scarring (see Figure 3-18 ■) The cirrhotic liver is enlarged, and its function is severely impaired. There is nausea and vomiting, weakness, and jaundice. Cirrhosis is caused by alcoholism, viral hepatitis, or chronic obstruction of the bile ducts. Severe cirrhosis can progress to liver failure. Treatment: Correct the underlying cause.	**cirrhosis** (sih-ROH-sis) **cirrh/o-** *yellow* **-osis** *condition; abnormal condition; process*

Figure 3-18 ■ **Fatty liver disease and cirrhosis of the liver.**
The liver on the left is normal. The liver in the center shows fatty liver disease, which is common in alcoholics because the sugar in alcohol is converted to triglycerides (fats) and stored in the liver. Diabetes mellitus and lipid (fat) disorders also cause this yellow, fatty appearance. The liver on the right shows cirrhosis. It is deformed with nodules and scar tissue that affect liver function.

Word or Phrase	Description	Word Building
hepatitis	Inflammation and infection of the liver from the hepatitis virus. There is weakness, anorexia, nausea, fever, dark urine, and jaundice. It is also known as **viral hepatitis**. *(continued)*	**hepatitis** (HEP-ah-TY-tis) **hepat/o-** *liver* **-itis** *inflammation of; infection of* **viral** (VY-ral) **vir/o-** *virus* **-al** *pertaining to*

DID YOU KNOW?

The leading cause of acute liver failure in the United States is acetaminophen overdose. Acetaminophen has been sold as an over-the-counter drug since 1970. Its most popular brand name is Tylenol.

Activity

Hepatitis Study

Divide the class into five groups. Each group is assigned one type of hepatitis (Hepatitis A, B, C, D, or E). Have each group present the following information: symptoms of the disease, method of transmission, degree of damage, prognosis, and treatment. Write the information in a table drawn on the board. Along a vertical column on the left, list the five types of hepatitis. In a horizontal row across the top, list the categories of information.

Word or Phrase	Description	Word Building
hepatitis *(continued)*		

A Closer Look

Hepatitis is the most common chronic liver disease. There are five types of hepatitis.

- **Hepatitis A** is an acute but short-lived infection and most persons recover completely. There is no chronic form. It is caused by exposure to water or food that is contaminated with feces from a person who is infected with the hepatitis A virus (HAV). It is also known as **infectious hepatitis.** Treatment: Vaccination to prevent hepatitis A.
- **Hepatitis B** is an acute infection, but many persons recover completely. When it is chronic, there may be no symptoms for 20 years. During that time, however, the infected person is a carrier and can infect others. Hepatitis B is caused by exposure to the blood of a person who is already infected with the hepatitis B virus (HBV) (see Figure 3-19 ■). It is also spread during sexual activity by contact with saliva and vaginal secretions. An infected mother can pass hepatitis B to her fetus before birth or when breastfeeding. It is also known as **serum hepatitis.** Treatment: Vaccination. Healthcare workers are vaccinated because of their constant exposure to blood and body fluids.
- **Hepatitis C** begins as an acute infection that continues as a chronic infection. It is caused by exposure to contaminated needles or to the blood of a person who is already infected with the hepatitis C virus (HCV). Hepatitis C is not readily transmitted by sexual activity or from a mother to her fetus. Chronic hepatitis C is the main cause of chronic liver disease, cirrhosis, and liver cancer. Treatment: Antiviral drugs.
- **Hepatitis D** is a secondary infection caused by a mutated (changed) hepatitis virus. It only develops in patients who already have hepatitis B. It is also known as **delta hepatitis.**
- **Hepatitis E** is similar to hepatitis A, but rarely occurs in the United States.

infectious (in-FEK-shus)
 infect/o- *disease within*
 -ous *pertaining to*

serum (SEER-um)
Serum is the fluid portion of the blood (without the cells and clotting factors).

delta (DEL-tah)

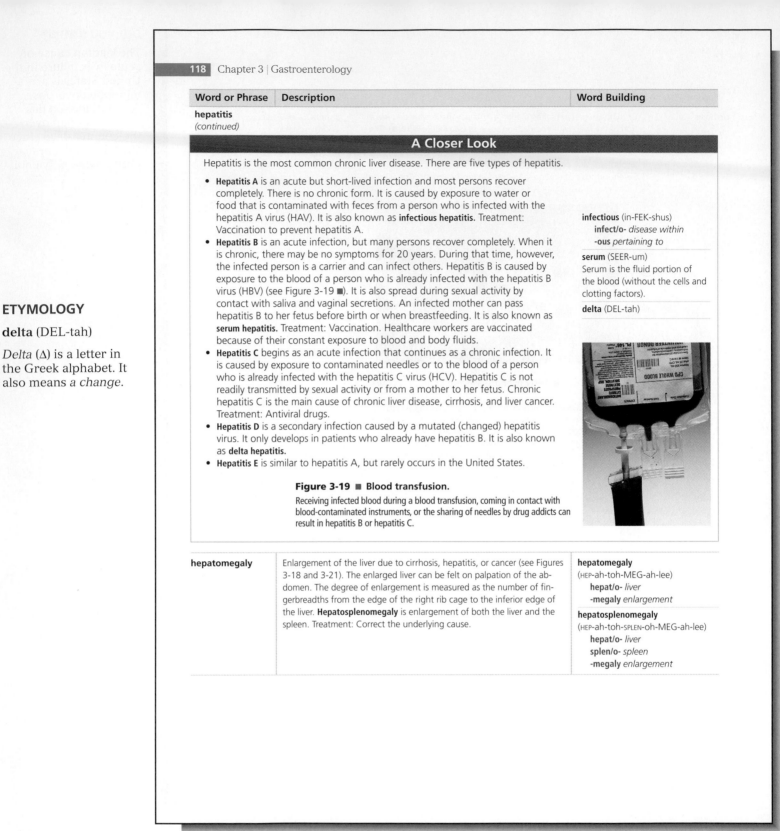

Figure 3-19 ■ Blood transfusion.
Receiving infected blood during a blood transfusion, coming in contact with blood-contaminated instruments, or the sharing of needles by drug addicts can result in hepatitis B or hepatitis C.

Word or Phrase	Description	Word Building
hepatomegaly	Enlargement of the liver due to cirrhosis, hepatitis, or cancer (see Figures 3-18 and 3-21). The enlarged liver can be felt on palpation of the abdomen. The degree of enlargement is measured as the number of fingerbreadths from the edge of the right rib cage to the inferior edge of the liver. **Hepatosplenomegaly** is enlargement of both the liver and the spleen. Treatment: Correct the underlying cause.	**hepatomegaly** (HEP-ah-toh-MEG-ah-lee) **hepat/o-** *liver* **-megaly** *enlargement* **hepatosplenomegaly** (HEP-ah-toh-SPLEN-oh-MEG-ah-lee) **hepat/o-** *liver* **splen/o-** *spleen* **-megaly** *enlargement*

ETYMOLOGY

delta (DEL-tah)

Delta (Δ) is a letter in the Greek alphabet. It also means *a change.*

Talking Point

Hepatitis

Hepatitis C is the leading cause of liver failure and the major reason for liver transplants. About 25,000 Americans die each year while waiting for a liver transplant. This is partly due to the lack of available donor livers and to the fact that there is no way to mechanically sustain life as can be done with hemodialysis for a patient with kidney failure. One possible solution is surgery to split the liver of a living donor and give half to the patient in liver failure. This has been done successfully, and both the donated liver and the original liver continue to function while growing back to a normal size within the abdominal cavity.

Source: ScienCentralNews at www.sciencentral.com, June 29, 2004.

Word or Phrase	Description	Word Building

jaundice	Yellowish discoloration of the skin and whites of the eyes (the sclerae) (see Figure 3-20 ■). There is an increased level of unconjugated bilirubin in the blood. This bilirubin enters the tissues, giving them a yellow color. Jaundice occurs:
	
	1. If the liver is too diseased to conjugate bilirubin.
	2. If the liver is too immature to conjugate bilirubin. This occurs in premature newborns.
	3. If there is too much unconjugated bilirubin in the blood because of the destruction of large numbers of red blood cells.
	4. If a gallstone is obstructing the flow of bile in the bile ducts (**obstructive jaundice**).
	
	Treatment: Correct the underlying disease.
		jaundice (JAWN-dis)
		  jaund/o- *yellow*
		  -ice *state; quality*
		
		obstructive (awb-STRUK-tiv)
		  obstruct/o- *blocked by a barrier*
		  -ive *pertaining to*

Figure 3-20 ■ Jaundice.
Jaundice can be seen as a yellow discoloration of the whites of the eyes (sclerae). The skin is also yellow, but skin pigmentation masks this to some extent.

A Closer Look

Bilirubin is produced when old red blood cells are broken down by the spleen. This is unconjugated (unjoined) bilirubin. The liver joins this bilirubin to another substance to make conjugated (joined) bilirubin, which is used to make bile. When the liver is damaged, the amount of unconjugated bilirubin in the blood increases. When gallstones obstruct the flow of bile, conjugated bilirubin leaves the bile and moves into the blood.

Word or Phrase	Description	Word Building

liver cancer	Cancerous tumor of the liver (see Figure 3-21 ■). This is usually a secondary cancer that began in another place and spread (metastasized) to the liver. It is also known as a **hepatoma** or **hepatocellular carcinoma**. Treatment: Surgery to remove the tumor; chemotherapy.	**hepatoma** (HEP-ah-TOH-mah)
		  hepat/o- *liver*
		  -oma *tumor; mass*
		
		hepatocellular (HEP-ah-toh-SEL-yoo-lar)
		  hepat/o- *liver*
		  cellul/o- *cell*
		  -ar *pertaining to*
		
		carcinoma (KAR-sih-NOH-mah)
		  carcin/o- *cancer*
		  -oma *tumor; mass*

Figure 3-21 ■ Liver cancer.
This colorized computed tomography (CT) scan of the abdomen shows an enlarged (yellow) liver with several large, dark areas where cancer has spread.

ETYMOLOGY

The yellow discoloration of the whites of the eyes is known as *scleral icterus. Icterus* is a Greek word that means *jaundice.*

Talking Point

Gastrointestinal Disease Words

Some medical words have a musical quality that sounds something like the thing they represent (like the word "boom"). Pronounce these gastrointestinal disease words and write them on the board. Then give the meanings.

borborygmus	[bohr-boh-RIG-mus]
singultus	[sing-GUL-tus]
intussuception	[in-tus-suh-SEP-shun]

Source: Adapted from Ellen Drake, "Using Storytelling to Teach and Learn Medical Terminology," *Perspectives on the Medical Transcription Profession,* Summer 2002, pp. 10–12.

Gallbladder and Bile Ducts

Word or Phrase	Description	Word Building

cholangitis	Acute or chronic inflammation of the bile ducts because of cirrhosis or gallstones. Treatment: Correct the underlying disease.	**cholangitis** (KOH-lan-JY-tis)
		  cholangi/o- *bile duct*
		  -itis *inflammation of; infection of*
		Delete the duplicate *i* when building the word.

cholecystitis	Acute or chronic inflammation of the gallbladder. Acute cholecystitis occurs when a gallstone blocks the cystic duct of the gallbladder. When the gallbladder contracts, the duct spasms, causing severe pain (**biliary colic**). Chronic cholecystitis occurs when a gallstone partially blocks the cystic duct, causing backup of bile and thickening of the gallbladder wall. Treatment: Avoid fatty foods that cause the gallbladder to contract. Drugs to dissolve the gallstone. Surgery to remove the gallbladder (cholecystectomy).	**cholecystitis** (KOH-lee-sis-TY-tis)
		  cholecyst/o- *gallbladder*
		  -itis *inflammation of; infection of*

cholelithiasis	One or more gallstones in the gallbladder (see Figure 3-22 ■). When the bile is too concentrated, it forms a thick sediment (sludge) that gradually becomes gallstones. Cholelithiasis causes mild symptoms or can cause severe biliary colic when the gallbladder contracts or when a gallstone becomes lodged in a bile duct. **Choledocholithiasis** is a gallstone that is stuck in the common bile duct (see Figure 3-23 ■). Treatment: Avoid fatty foods that cause the gallbladder to contract. Drugs to dissolve the gallstone. Surgery to remove the gallbladder (cholecystectomy) or to remove a gallstone from the common bile duct (choledocholithotomy).	**cholelithiasis** (KOH-lee-lih-THY-ah-sis)
		  chol/e- *bile; gall*
		  lith/o- *stone*
		  -iasis *state of; process of*
		choledocholithiasis
		(koh-LED-oh-koh-lith-EYE-ah-sis)
		  choledoch/o- *common bile duct*
		  lith/o- *stone*
		  -iasis *state of; process of*

Figure 3-22 ■ **Cholelithiasis.**
This patient's gallbladder was removed during surgery. When it was opened by the pathologist, it contained numerous small and large gallstones.

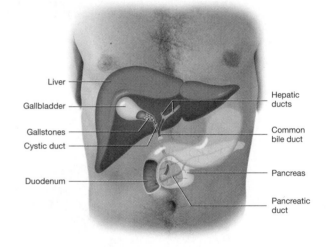

Figure 3-23 ■ **Gallstones in the biliary and pancreatic ducts.**
A gallstone in the cystic duct causes bile to back up into the gallbladder. A gallstone in the proximal common bile duct causes bile to back up into the gallbladder and liver. A gallstone in the distal common bile duct keeps pancreatic digestive enzymes from entering the duodenum.

Pancreas

Word or Phrase	Description	Word Building

pancreatic cancer	Cancerous tumor (**adenocarcinoma**) of the pancreas. Most patients are in the advanced stage when they are diagnosed and so survival is usually less than one year. Treatment: Chemotherapy; surgery to remove the tumor.	**adenocarcinoma**
		(AD-eh-noh-KAR-sih-NOH-mah)
		   aden/o- *gland*
		   carcin/o- *cancer*
		   -oma *tumor; mass*

pancreatitis	Inflammation or infection of the pancreas. There is abdominal pain, nausea, and vomiting. Inflammation occurs when a gallstone blocks the lower common bile duct and pancreatic enzymes back up into the pancreas. Inflammation of the pancreas can also be due to chronic alcoholism. Infection in the pancreas is caused by bacteria or viruses. Treatment: Stop drinking alcohol. Antibiotic drugs to treat a bacterial infection. Surgery to remove a gallstone (choledocholithotomy).	**pancreatitis** (PAN-kree-ah-TY-tis)
		   pancreat/o- *pancreas*
		   -itis *inflammation of; infection of*

Activity

Look It Up

Instruct students to obtain information from the American Cancer Society regarding cancers that affect the gastrointestinal organs such as colon cancer, stomach cancer, and pancreatic cancer.

Laboratory and Diagnostic Procedures

Blood Tests

Word or Phrase	Description	Word Building
albumin	Test for albumin, the major protein molecule in the blood. Because albumin is produced by the liver, liver disease results in a low albumin level. The albumin level is also low in patients with malnutrition from poor protein intake.	**albumin** (al-BYOO-min)
alkaline phosphatase (ALP)	Test for the enzyme alkaline phosphatase that is found in both liver cells and bone cells. An elevated blood level is due to liver disease or bone disease.	**alkaline phosphatase** (AL-kah-lin FAWS-fah-tays)
ALT and AST	Test for the enzymes alanine transaminase (ALT) and aspartate transaminase (AST), which are mainly found in the liver. Elevated blood levels occur when damaged liver cells release these enzymes. Formerly known as **SGPT** and **SGOT.**	
bilirubin	Test for unconjugated, conjugated, and total bilirubin levels. These levels are abnormal when there is liver disease or gallstones. Conjugated bilirubin is also known as **direct bilirubin** because it reacts directly with the reagent used to perform the lab test. Unconjugated bilirubin or **indirect bilirubin** only reacts when another substance is added to the reagent.	**bilirubin** (BIL-ih-ROO-bin) **bili/o-** *bile; gall* **rub/o-** *red* **-in** *a substance*
GGT	Test for the enzyme gamma-glutamyl transpeptidase (GGT or GGTP), which is mainly found in the liver. An elevated blood level occurs when damaged liver cells release this enzyme into the blood.	
liver function tests (LFTs)	Panel of individual blood tests performed at the same time to give a comprehensive picture of liver function. It includes albumin, bilirubin, ALT, AST, and GGT, as well as prothrombin time (to evaluate blood clotting factors produced by the liver).	

Gastric and Feces Specimen Tests

Word or Phrase	Description	Word Building
CLO test	Rapid screening test to detect the presence of the bacterium *Helicobacter pylori.* A biopsy of the patient's gastric mucosa is placed in urea. If *H. pylori* bacteria are present, they metabolize the urea to ammonia, and ammonia changes the color of the test pad.	**CLO** (kloh) *CLO* stands for *Campylobacter-like organism* (because *H. pylori* used to be categorized with the genus Campylobacter).
culture and sensitivity (C&S)	Diagnostic test of a culture that determines which bacterium is causing an intestinal infection and a sensitivity test to determine which antibiotic drugs it is sensitive to. The patient's feces are swabbed onto a culture dish that contains a nutrient medium for growing bacteria. After the bacterium grows, it can be identified by the appearance of the colonies. Then disks of antibiotic drugs are placed in the culture dish. If the bacteria are resistant to that antibiotic drug, there will only be a small zone of inhibition (no growth) around it. If the bacteria are sensitive to that antibiotic drug, there will be a medium or large zone of inhibition around that disk.	**sensitivity** (SEN-sih-TIV-ih-tee) **sensitiv/o-** *affected by; sensitive to* **-ity** *state; condition*

Word or Phrase	Description	Word Building
fecal occult blood test	Diagnostic test for occult (hidden) blood in the feces. The feces are mixed with the chemical reagent guaiac. This is also known as a **stool guaiac test**. If blood is present, the guaiac will turn a blue color (guaiac-positive). Hemoccult and Coloscreen cards can be purchased by consumers for home testing. The results of these tests are heme positive or heme negative because they detect the heme molecule of hemoglobin from the blood.	**occult** (oh-KULT) **guaiac** (GWY-ak)

gastric analysis	Diagnostic test to determine the amount of hydrochloric acid in the stomach. A nasogastric (NG) tube is inserted, and gastric fluid is collected. Then a drug is given to stimulate acid production, and another sample is collected.	**gastric** (GAS-trik)
		   gastr/o- *stomach*
		   -ic *pertaining to*

ova and parasites (O&P)	Diagnostic test to determine if there is a parasitic infection in the gastrointestinal tract. Ova are the eggs of parasitic worms. They can be seen in the feces or by examining a sample under a microscope.	**ovum** (OH-vum) **ova** (OH-va) *Ovum* is a Latin singular noun. Form the plural by changing -*um* to -*a*. **parasite** (PAIR-ah-site)

Radiologic Procedures

barium enema (BE)	Procedure that uses liquid radiopaque contrast medium (barium) instilled into the rectum and colon (see Figure 3-24 ■). Barium outlines and coats the walls, and an x-ray is then taken. This test is used to identify polyps, diverticula, ulcerative colitis, and colon cancer.	**barium** (BAIR-ee-um) **enema** (EN-eh-mah)

Figure 3-24 ■ **Barium enema.**
Barium contrast medium inserted through the rectum fills the rectum, sigmoid colon, descending colon, transverse colon, and ascending colon on this x-ray.

ETYMOLOGY

Occult comes from a Latin word meaning *to hide.*

Guaiac is a resin that comes from the tropical plant Guaiacum.

ETYMOLOGY

Parasite comes from a Greek word meaning *a guest.*

Enema comes from a Greek word meaning *to throw into.*

Word or Phrase	Description	Word Building
cholangiography	Procedure that uses a contrast dye to outline the bile ducts. Then an x-ray is taken to show stones in the gallbladder and bile ducts or thickening of the gallbladder wall. The x-ray image is a **cholangiogram.** For an **intravenous cholangiography (IVC),** the contrast dye is injected intravenously, travels through the blood to the liver, and is excreted with bile into the gallbladder. For a **percutaneous transhepatic cholangiography (PTC),** a needle is passed through the abdominal wall, and the contrast dye is injected into the liver. For an **endoscopic retrograde cholangiopancreatography (ERCP),** the contrast dye is injected going backward (in the opposite direction of the flow of bile and enzymes) to visualize the common bile duct and pancreatic duct (see Figure 3-25 ■). 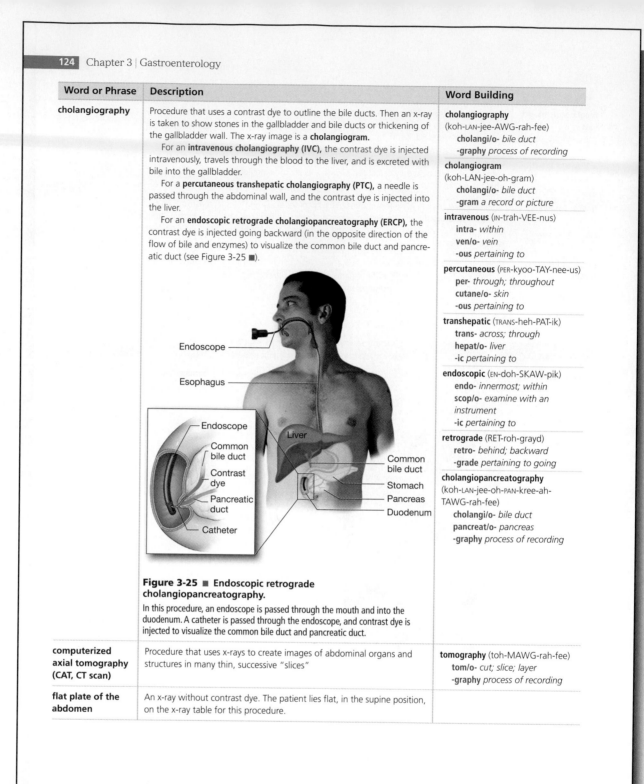 **Figure 3-25 ■ Endoscopic retrograde cholangiopancreatography.** In this procedure, an endoscope is passed through the mouth and into the duodenum. A catheter is passed through the endoscope, and contrast dye is injected to visualize the common bile duct and pancreatic duct.	**cholangiography** (koh-LAN-jee-AWG-rah-fee) cholangi/o- *bile duct* -graphy *process of recording* **cholangiogram** (koh-LAN-jee-oh-gram) cholangi/o- *bile duct* -gram *a record or picture* **intravenous** (IN-trah-VEE-nus) intra- *within* ven/o- *vein* -ous *pertaining to* **percutaneous** (PER-kyoo-TAY-nee-us) per- *through; throughout* cutane/o- *skin* -ous *pertaining to* **transhepatic** (TRANS-heh-PAT-ik) trans- *across; through* hepat/o- *liver* -ic *pertaining to* **endoscopic** (EN-doh-SKAW-pik) endo- *innermost; within* scop/o- *examine with an instrument* -ic *pertaining to* **retrograde** (RET-roh-grayd) retro- *behind; backward* -grade *pertaining to going* **cholangiopancreatography** (koh-LAN-jee-oh-PAN-kree-ah-TAWG-rah-fee) cholangi/o- *bile duct* pancreat/o- *pancreas* -graphy *process of recording*
computerized axial tomography (CAT, CT scan)	Procedure that uses x-rays to create images of abdominal organs and structures in many thin, successive "slices"	**tomography** (toh-MAWG-rah-fee) tom/o- *cut; slice; layer* -graphy *process of recording*
flat plate of the abdomen	An x-ray without contrast dye. The patient lies flat, in the supine position, on the x-ray table for this procedure.	

Talking Point

Medical Humor

Ask students if they would like to have a sneak peek at one of the questions that will be on the test for this chapter. When they say "Yes," then say: There is only one question on the test. Here it is: "On your desk, you will find a scalpel and sutures. Remove your own appendix, and then close the incision. Your suturing technique will be checked for neatness."

Word or Phrase	Description	Word Building

gallbladder ultrasound	Procedure that uses ultra high-frequency sound waves to create images of the gallbladder. It is used to identify gallstones and thickening of the gallbladder wall. The image is a **gallbladder sonogram.**	**ultrasound** (UL-trah-sound)
		 sonogram (SAWN-oh-gram)
		   son/o- *sound*
		   -gram *a record or picture*

magnetic resonance imaging (MRI scan)	Procedure that uses a strong magnetic field to align protons in the atoms of the patient's body. The protons emit signals to form images of abdominal organs and structures as thin, successive "slices."	**magnetic** (mag-NET-ik)
		   magnet/o- *magnet*
		   -ic *pertaining to*

oral cholecysto-graphy (OCG)	Procedure that uses tablets of radiopaque contrast dye taken orally. The tablets dissolve in the intestine. The contrast dye is absorbed into the blood, travels to the liver, and is excreted with bile into the gallbladder. An x-ray is taken to identify stones in the gallbladder and biliary ducts or thickening of the gallbladder wall. The x-ray image is a **cholecystogram.**	**cholecystography** (KOH-lee-sis-TAWG-rah-fee)
		   cholecyst/o- *gallbladder*
		   -graphy *process of recording*
		 cholecystogram (KOH-lee-SIS-toh-gram)
		   cholecyst/o- *gallbladder*
		   -gram *a record or picture*

upper gastro-intestinal series (UGI)	Procedure that uses a liquid radiopaque contrast medium (barium) that is swallowed (a barium meal). Barium coats and outlines the walls of the esophagus, stomach, and duodenum. It is also known as a **barium swallow.** Fluoroscopy (a continuously moving x-ray image on a screen) is used to follow the barium through the small intestine. This is a **small bowel follow-through.** Individual x-rays are taken at specific times throughout the procedure (see Figure 19-4). This test identifies ulcers, tumors, or obstruction in the esophagus, stomach, and small intestine.	

ETYMOLOGY

Ultrasound is a combination of the prefix *ultra-* (beyond; higher) and the word *sound*.

MEDIA RESOURCES

See the PowerPoint presentation on www.myhealthprofessionskit.com for an animation and a video on the following topics covered in this chapter:

- MRIs
- Ultrasound

Medical and Surgical Procedures

Medical Procedures

Word or Phrase	Description	Word Building
insertion of nasogastric tube (NG tube)	Procedure to insert a long, flexible **nasogastric tube** through the nostril into the stomach. It is used to drain secretions from the stomach or give feedings to the patient on a temporary basis (see Figure 3-26 ■).	**nasogastric** (NAY-zoh-GAS-trik) **nas/o-** *nose* **gastr/o-** *stomach* **-ic** *pertaining to*

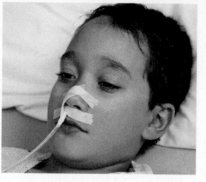

Did You Know?

The first nasogastric tube, developed in the late 1700s, was constructed from eel skin. It was used for several weeks to feed a patient who could not eat.

Figure 3-26 ■ Nasogastric tube.
This patient has a nasogastric (NG) tube. It was inserted into one nostril and, as he swallowed, it was advanced through the esophagus and into the stomach. Only liquid feedings or liquid drugs can be given through an NG tube.

Surgical Procedures

Word or Phrase	Description	Word Building
abdominocentesis	Procedure to remove fluid from the abdomen using a needle and a vacuum container. It is done to relieve abdominal pressure from fluid produced by ascites. It is also done to see if there are cancer cells in the peritoneal fluid or to see if there is blood in the peritoneal fluid after abdominal trauma.	**abdominocentesis** (ab-DAWM-ih-noh-sen-TEE-sis) **abdomin/o-** *abdomen* **-centesis** *procedure to puncture*
appendectomy	Procedure to remove the appendix because of appendicitis	**appendectomy** (AP-pen-DEK-toh-mee) **append/o-** *small structure hanging from a larger structure; appendix* **-ectomy** *surgical excision*
biopsy	Procedure to remove a small piece of tissue from an ulcer, polyp, mass, or tumor to look for abnormal or cancerous cells	**biopsy** (BY-awp-see) **bi/o-** *life; living organisms; living tissue* **-opsy** *process of viewing*
bowel resection and anastomosis	Procedure to remove a section of diseased intestine and rejoin the intestine. An end-to-end anastomosis joins the two cut ends together. An end-to-side anastomosis joins one end to the side of another segment.	**resection** (ree-SEK-shun) **resect/o-** *to cut out; remove* **-ion** *action; condition* **anastomosis** (ah-NAS-toh-MOH-sis) **anastom/o-** *create an opening between two structures* **-osis** *condition; abnormal condition; process*

Word or Phrase	Description	Word Building
cholecystectomy	Procedure to remove the gallbladder. This is done as a minimally invasive **laparoscopic cholecystectomy** that uses a **laparoscope** (see Figure 3-27 ■).	**cholecystectomy** (KOH-lee-sis-TEK-toh-mee) **cholecyst/o-** *gallbladder* **-ectomy** *surgical excision* **laparoscopic** (LAP-ah-roh-SKAWP-ik) **lapar/o-** *abdomen* **scop/o-** *examine with an instrument* **-ic** *pertaining to* **laparoscope** (LAP-ah-roh-skohp) **lapar/o-** *abdomen* **-scope** *instrument used to examine*

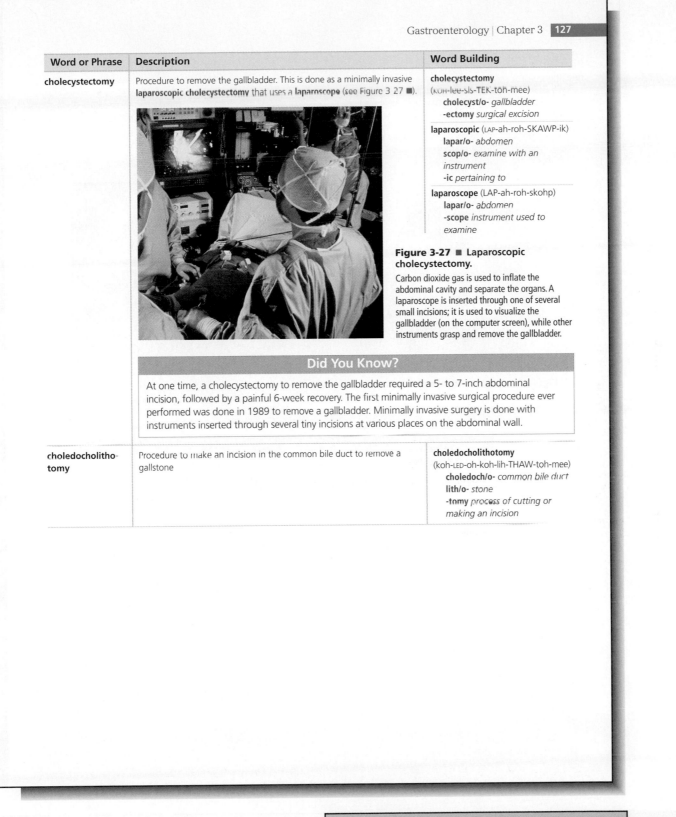

Figure 3-27 ■ Laparoscopic cholecystectomy.
Carbon dioxide gas is used to inflate the abdominal cavity and separate the organs. A laparoscope is inserted through one of several small incisions; it is used to visualize the gallbladder (on the computer screen), while other instruments grasp and remove the gallbladder.

Did You Know?

At one time, a cholecystectomy to remove the gallbladder required a 5- to 7-inch abdominal incision, followed by a painful 6-week recovery. The first minimally invasive surgical procedure ever performed was done in 1989 to remove a gallbladder. Minimally invasive surgery is done with instruments inserted through several tiny incisions at various places on the abdominal wall.

Word or Phrase	Description	Word Building
choledocholitho-tomy	Procedure to make an incision in the common bile duct to remove a gallstone	**choledocholithotomy** (koh-LED-oh-koh-lih-THAW-toh-mee) **choledoch/o-** *common bile duct* **lith/o-** *stone* **-tomy** *process of cutting or making an incision*

Talking Point

Abdominal Surgery

Discuss the innovations in abdominal surgery such as laparoscopic appendectomies, cholecystectomies and exploratory surgeries. Surgery no longer needs to be invasive and is often done on an outpatient basis.

Stoma is a Greek word meaning *a mouth*.

Word or Phrase	Description	Word Building

colostomy	Procedure to remove the diseased part of the colon and create a new opening in the abdominal wall where feces can leave the body (see Figure 3-28 ■). The colon is brought out through the abdominal wall. The edges of the colon are rolled to make a mouth (**stoma**) and sutured to the abdominal wall. The patient wears a plastic disposable pouch that adheres to the abdominal wall to collect feces. If part of the ileum and colon are removed and a stoma created, the procedure is known as an **ileostomy**.	**colostomy** (koh-LAWS-toh-mee)
		  col/o- *colon*
		  -stomy *surgically created opening*
		stoma (STOH-mah)
		ileostomy (IL-ee-AWS-toh-mee)
		  ile/o- *ileum*
		  -stomy *surgically created opening*

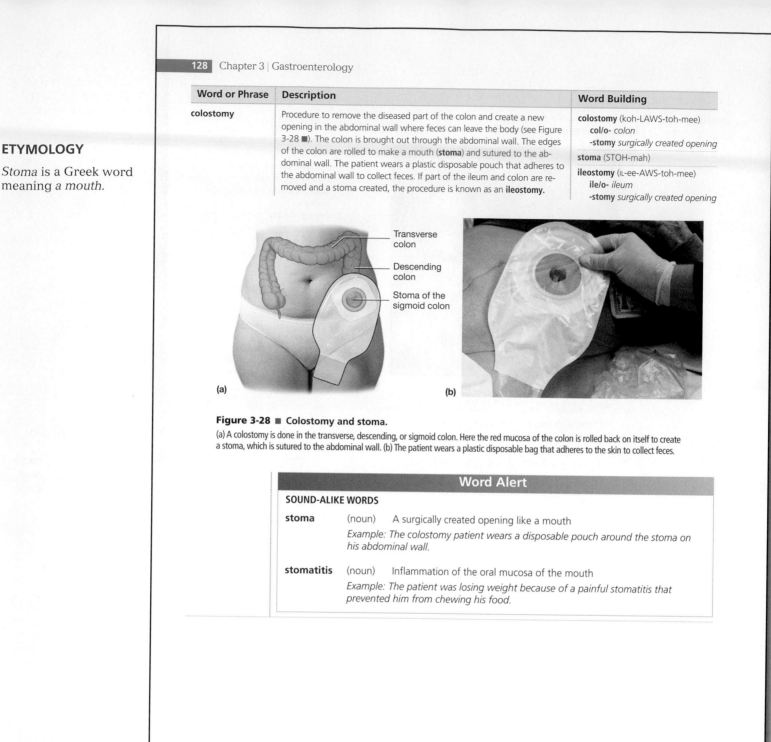

Transverse colon

Descending colon

Stoma of the sigmoid colon

(a)

(b)

Figure 3-28 ■ Colostomy and stoma.

(a) A colostomy is done in the transverse, descending, or sigmoid colon. Here the red mucosa of the colon is rolled back on itself to create a stoma, which is sutured to the abdominal wall. (b) The patient wears a plastic disposable bag that adheres to the skin to collect feces.

Word Alert

SOUND-ALIKE WORDS

stoma (noun) A surgically created opening like a mouth

Example: The colostomy patient wears a disposable pouch around the stoma on his abdominal wall.

stomatitis (noun) Inflammation of the oral mucosa of the mouth

Example: The patient was losing weight because of a painful stomatitis that prevented him from chewing his food.

Talking Point

Medical Humor

The amount of information in this chapter is substantial. I may not have succeeded in answering all your questions. Indeed, some of the answers only served to raise a whole new set of questions, some of which we didn't even know were questions! To sum it all up, in some ways you may feel confused, but you are now confused on a higher level and about more important things! (Adapted from a popular e-mail)

Word or Phrase	Description	Word Building
endoscopy	Procedure that uses an **endoscope** (a flexible, fiberoptic scope with a magnifying lens and a light source) to internally examine the gastrointestinal tract. An endoscopic procedure can be coupled with another procedure such as a biopsy or removal of a polyp.	**endoscopy** (en-DAWS-koh-pee) **endo-** *innermost; within* **-scopy** *process of using an instrument to examine* **endoscope** (EN-doh-skohp) **endo-** *innermost; within* **-scope** *instrument used to examine*

A Closer Look

These procedures use an endoscope inserted through the nose or mouth.

- **esophagoscopy:** visualization and examination of the esophagus
- **gastroscopy:** visualization and examination of the stomach (after the endoscope first passes through the esophagus)
- **esophagogastroduodenoscopy (EGD):** visualization and examination of the esophagus first, followed by the stomach, and then the duodenum

The ileum, cecum, and ascending colon cannot be visualized with endoscopy. Instead, the patient swallows a capsule that contains a small camera. It uses wireless technology to transmit pictures until it is excreted from the body.

These procedures use an endoscope inserted through the rectum.

- **sigmoidoscopy:** visualization and examination of the rectum and sigmoid colon using a sigmoidoscope
- **colonoscopy:** visualization and examination of the entire colon after the colonoscope is passed through the rectum (see Figure 3-29 ■)

esophagoscopy
(ee-SAWF-ah-GAWS-koh-pee)
esophag/o- *esophagus*
-scopy *process of using an instrument to examine*

gastroscopy (gas-TRAWS-koh-pee)
gastr/o- *stomach*
-scopy *process of using an instrument to examine*

esophagogastroduodenoscopy
(ee-SAWF-ah-goh-GAS-troh-DOO-oh-den-AWS-koh-pee)
esophag/o- *esophagus*
gastr/o- *stomach*
duoden/o- *duodenum*
-scopy *process of using an instrument to examine*

sigmoidoscopy
(SIG-moy-DAWS-koh-pee)
sigmoid/o- *sigmoid colon*
-scopy *process of using an instrument to examine*

colonoscopy (KOH-lon-AWS-koh-pee)
colon/o- *colon*
-scopy *process of using an instrument to examine*

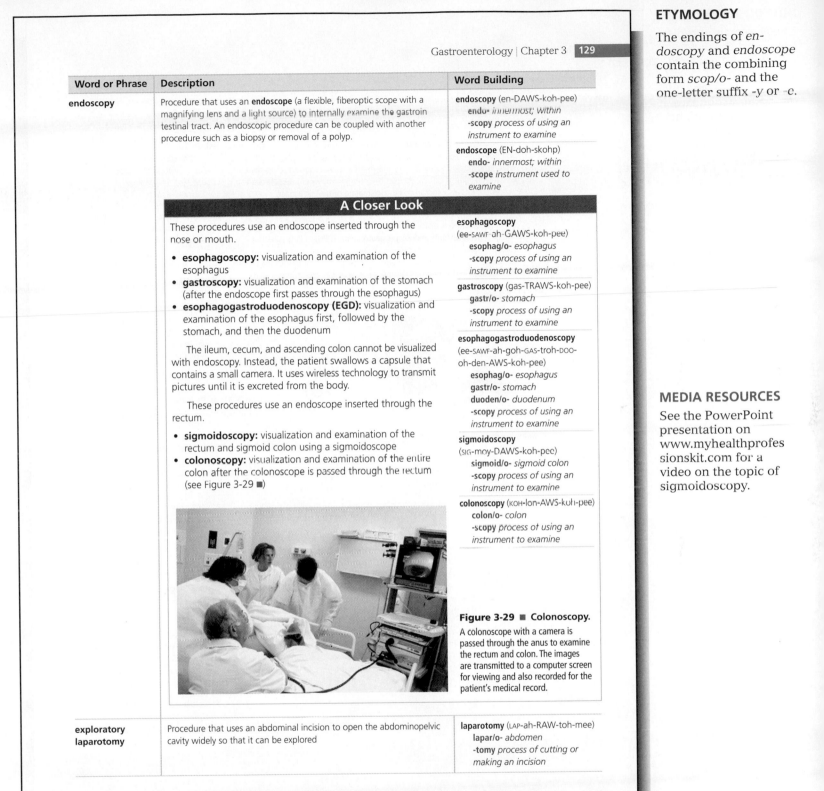

Figure 3-29 ■ Colonoscopy.
A colonoscope with a camera is passed through the anus to examine the rectum and colon. The images are transmitted to a computer screen for viewing and also recorded for the patient's medical record.

| exploratory laparotomy | Procedure that uses an abdominal incision to open the abdominopelvic cavity widely so that it can be explored | **laparotomy** (LAP-ah-RAW-toh-mee)
lapar/o- *abdomen*
-tomy *process of cutting or making an incision* |

ETYMOLOGY

The endings of *endoscopy* and *endoscope* contain the combining form *scop/o-* and the one-letter suffix *-y* or *-e*.

MEDIA RESOURCES

See the PowerPoint presentation on www.myhealthprofessionskit.com for a video on the topic of sigmoidoscopy.

Word or Phrase	Description	Word Building
gastrectomy	Procedure to remove all or part of the stomach because of a cancerous or benign tumor	**gastrectomy** (gas-TREK-toh-mee) **gastr/o-** *stomach* **-ectomy** *surgical excision*
gastroplasty	Procedure to treat severe obesity. Staples are used to make a small stomach pouch. A gastroplasty can be combined with a gastric bypass in which the stapled stomach pouch is anastomosed (connected) to the cut end of the jejunum. This bypasses the duodenum, where most fats are absorbed. It is also known as **gastric stapling** or **gastric bypass.**	**gastroplasty** (GAS-troh-PLAS-tee) **gastr/o-** *stomach* **-plasty** *process of reshaping by surgery*
gastrostomy	Procedure to create a temporary or permanent opening from the abdominal wall into the stomach to insert a gastrostomy feeding tube. For a **percutaneous endoscopic gastrostomy (PEG)**, a PEG tube is inserted through the abdominal wall. Then under visual guidance from an endoscope that was previously passed through the mouth into the stomach, a catheter inside the PEG tube is positioned in the stomach (see Figure 3-30 ■). Abdominal wall Skin Stomach PEG tube **Figure 3-30** ■ **PEG tube.** This permanent feeding tube is inserted during a percutaneous endoscopic gastrostomy.	**gastrostomy** (gas-TRAWS-toh-mee) **gastr/o-** *stomach* **-stomy** *surgically created opening* **percutaneous** (PER-kyoo-TAY-nee-us) **per-** *through; throughout* **cutane/o-** *skin* **-ous** *pertaining to* **endoscopic** (EN-doh-SKAW-pik) **endo-** *innermost; within* **scop/o-** *examine with an instrument* **-ic** *pertaining to*
hemorrhoid-ectomy	Procedure to remove hemorrhoids from the rectum or around the anus	**hemorrhoidectomy** (HEM-oh-roy-DEK-toh-mee) **hemorrhoid/o-** *hemorrhoid* **-ectomy** *surgical excision*
herniorrhaphy	Procedure that uses sutures to close a defect in the muscle wall where there is a hernia	**herniorrhaphy** (HER-nee-OR-ah-fee) **herni/o-** *hernia* **-rrhaphy** *procedure of suturing*
jejunostomy	Procedure to create a temporary or permanent opening from the abdominal wall into the jejunum through which to insert a jejunostomy feeding tube. For a **percutaneous endoscopic jejunostomy (PEJ),** a PEJ tube is inserted through the abdominal wall. Then under visual guidance from an endoscope that was previously passed through the mouth, the PEJ tube is positioned in the jejunum.	**jejunostomy** (JEH-joo-NAWS-toh-mee) **jejun/o-** *jejunum* **-stomy** *surgically created opening*
liver transplantation	Procedure to remove a severely damaged liver from a patient with end-stage liver disease and insert a new liver from a donor. The patient (the recipient) is matched by blood type and tissue type to the donor. Liver transplant patients must take immunosuppressant drugs for the rest of their lives to keep their bodies from rejecting the foreign tissue that is their new liver.	**transplantation** (TRANS-plan-TAY-shun) **transplant/o-** *move something to another place* **-ation** *a process; being or having*
polypectomy	Surgical excision of polyps from the colon using forceps	**polypectomy** (PAWL-ih-PEK-toh-mee) **polyp/o-** *polyp* **-ectomy** *surgical excision*

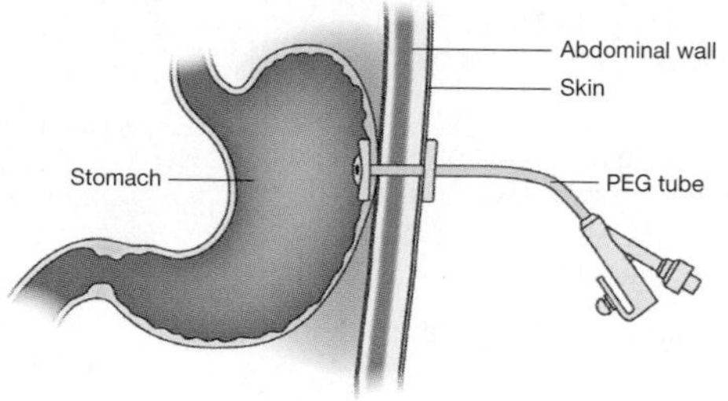

Drug Categories

These categories of drugs are used to treat gastrointestinal diseases and conditions. The most common generic and trade name drugs in each category are listed.

Category	Indication	Examples	Word Building
antacid drugs	Treat heartburn and peptic ulcer disease by neutralizing acid in the stomach	Maalox, Mylanta, Tums	**antacid** (ant-AS-id) *Antacid* is a combination of *anti-* (against) and the word *acid*. The *i* in *anti-* is deleted.
antibiotic drugs	Treat gastrointestinal infections caused by bacteria, including *Helicobacter pylori*. Antibiotic drugs are not effective against viral gastrointestinal infections.	amoxicillin (Amoxil), ciprofloxacin (Cipro), doxycycline (Vibramycin), Helidac (bismuth, metronidazole, tetracycline)	**antibiotic** (AN-tee-by-AWT-ik) (AN-tih-by-AWT-ik) **anti-** *against* **bi/o-** *life; living organisms; living tissue* **-tic** *pertaining to*
antidiarrheal drugs	Treat diarrhea. They slow peristalsis and this increases water absorption from the feces.	loperamide (Imodium), Lomotil (atropine, diphenoxylate)	**antidiarrheal** (AN-tee-DY-ah-REE-al) **anti-** *against* **dia-** *complete; completely through* **-rrhe/o-** *flow; discharge* **-al** *pertaining to*
antiemetic drugs	Treat nausea and vomiting and motion sickness	dimenhydrinate (Dramamine), meclizine (Antivert), prochlorperazine (Compazine)	**antiemetic** (AN-tee-eh-MET-ik) **anti-** *against* **emet/o-** *to vomit* **-ic** *pertaining to*
H₂ blocker drugs	Treat peptic ulcers by blocking H_2 (histamine 2) receptors in the stomach that trigger the release of hydrochloric acid	cimetidine (Tagamet), famotidine (Pepcid), ranitidine (Zantac)	
laxative drugs	Treat constipation by softening the stool, adding dietary fiber, or directly stimulating the intestinal mucosa	bisacodyl (Dulcolax), docusate (Colace, Surfak), psyllium (Fiberall, Metamucil)	**laxative** (LAK-sah-tiv)
proton pump inhibitor drugs	Treat heartburn, peptic ulcers, and gastroesophageal reflux disease (GERD) by blocking the final step in the production of hydrochloric acid	esomeprazole (Nexium), omeprazole (Prilosec)	

Did You Know?

A **suppository** is a bullet-shaped capsule that contains a drug. It is inserted into the rectum, where it melts and releases the drug.

suppository (SOO-PAWZ-ih-TOR-ee)
supposit/o- *placed beneath*
-ory *having the function of*

TEACHING STRATEGY
Stress the importance of learning abbreviations and their full meanings.

Abbreviations

ABD	abdomen		**LFTs**	liver function tests
a.c.	before meals (Latin, *ante cibum*)		**LLQ**	left lower quadrant
ALP	alkaline phosphatase		**LUQ**	left upper quadrant
ALT	alanine aminotransferase		**N&V**	nausea and vomiting
AST	aspartate aminotransferase		**NG**	nasogastric
BE	barium enema		**NPO**	nothing by mouth (Latin, *nil per os*)
BM	bowel movement		**(n.p.o.)**	
BRBPR	bright red blood per rectum		**OCG**	oral cholecystography
BS	bowel sounds		**O&P**	ova and parasites
CBD	common bile duct		**p.c.**	after meals (Latin, *post cibum*)
EGD	esophagogastroduodenoscopy		**PEG**	percutaneous endoscopic gastrostomy
ERCP	endoscopic retrograde cholangiopancreatography		**PEJ**	percutaneous endoscopic jejunostomy
GERD	gastroesophageal reflux disease		**PO (p.o.)**	by mouth (Latin, *per os*)
GI	gastrointestinal		**PTC**	percutaneous transhepatic cholangiography
HAV	hepatitis A virus		**PUD**	peptic ulcer disease
HBV	hepatitis B virus		**RLQ**	right lower quadrant
HCl	hydrochloric acid		**RUQ**	right upper quadrant
HCV	hepatitis C virus		**SGOT**	serum glutamic-oxaloacetic transaminase (older name for AST)
IBD	inflammatory bowel disease			
IBS	irritable bowel syndrome		**SGPT**	serum glutamic-pyruvic transaminase (older name for ALT)
IVC	intravenous cholangiography			
LES	lower esophageal sphincter		**UGI**	upper gastrointestinal (series)

Activity

Abbreviation Game

Give students three minutes to study the abbreviation list. Then divide the class into two, three, or four teams and have them stand in separate lines. The instructor writes a common gastrointestinal abbreviation on the board. The first person on Team 1 must indicate what the abbreviation stands for. If correct, that person moves to the back of the team line. The first person on Team 2 will then define the next abbreviation written on the board by the instructor. If correct, that person moves to the end of the team line, and so on. If at any point a team member misses an abbreviation, that person is out of the game. The next team is given an opportunity to define the abbreviation. The winners are the team with the most players left at the end of the game.

Students not answering the question can continue to study the abbreviations list in the textbook until it is their turn.

Word Alert

ABBREVIATIONS

Abbreviations are commonly used in all types of medical documents; however, they can mean different things to different people and their meanings can be misinterpreted. Always verify the meaning of an abbreviation.

BS means *bowel sounds*, but it also means *breath sounds*.

PUD means *peptic ulcer disease*, but when handwritten the *U* can look like a *V*; *PVD* means *peripheral vascular disease*.

Activity

Practice It

Have students write 10 sentences using 10 or more different abbreviations from the chapter.

Activity

Memory Aids

Have students create a "mnifty mnemonic device" memory aid in the form of a rhyme, a word, or an abbreviation that helps them remember something about this body system.

It's Greek to Me!

Did you notice that some words have two different combining forms? Combining forms from both Greek and Latin languages remain a part of medical language today.

Word	Greek	Latin	Medical Word Examples
abdomen	celi/o- lapar/o-	abdomin/o- ventr/o-	celiac trunk, celiac disease, abdominal laparoscopy, laparotomy, ventral
bile duct	cholangi/o- choledoch/o-	bili/o-	cholangitis, cholangiography, biliary choledocholithiasis, choledocholithotomy
digest	peps/o- pept/o-	digest/o-	pepsin, pepsinogen, digestive, digestion peptic
fats	steat/o-	lip/o-	steatorrhea, lipase
intestine	enter/o-	intestin/o-	enteropathy, gastroenteritis, gastroenterologist, gastroenterology, intestinal, gastrointestinal
mouth	stomat/o-	or/o-	stomatitis, oral
pass feces	chez/o-	fec/a-, fec/o-	hematochezia, fecalith, defecation
rectum	proct/o-	rect/o-	proctitis, rectal
saliva	sial/o-	saliv/o-	sialolith, sialolithiasis, salivary
tongue	gloss/o-	lingu/o-	glossitis, sublingual
umbilicus, navel	omphal/o-	umbilic/o-	omphalocele, umbilical

CAREER FOCUS

Meet Patricia, a medical assistant

"The best part of my job as a medical assistant is dealing with the patients. I love coming to work and doing it every day. It's just very fulfilling to me. I love helping people. I love talking to them. I love learning about their families, and that's what you find in this kind of practice. This is a huge clinic. It has internal medicine, pediatrics, OB/GYN, and plastic surgery. We have a specialty department with ears, nose, and throat doctors. We have optometry; we have physical therapy. I work with patients. I bring them in, I weigh them, take their blood pressure, find out what their problem is, write down their problem, and go to the physician and tell why the patient is here. I definitely think medical assistants are the first line of defense for the doctor. I bring everything to the doctor. We work as a team. We have a great rapport together and with our patients."

Medical assistants are allied health professionals who perform and document a variety of clinical and laboratory procedures and assist the physician during medical procedures in the office or clinic.

Gastroenterologists are physicians who practice in the medical specialty of gastroenterology. They diagnose and treat patients with diseases of the gastrointestinal system. Physicians can take additional training and become board certified in the subspecialty of pediatric gastroenterology. Cancerous tumors of the gastrointestinal system are treated medically by an **oncologist** or surgically by a general **surgeon**.

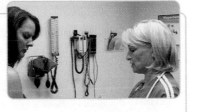

gastroenterologist
(GAS-troh EN ter-AWL-oh-jist)
  gastr/o- *stomach*
  enter/o- *intestine*
  log/o- *word; the study of*
  -ist *one who specializes in*

oncologist (ong-KAWL-oh-jist)
  onc/o- *tumor; mass*
  log/o- *word; the study of*
  -ist *one who specializes in*

surgeon (SER-jun)
  surg/o- *operative procedure*
  -eon *one who performs*

PEARSON myhealthprofessionskit™ To see Patricia's complete video profile, visit Medical Terminology Interactive at www.myhealthprofessionskit.com. Select this book, log in, and go to the 3rd floor of Pearson General Hospital. Enter the Laboratory, and click on the computer screen.

MEDIA RESOURCES

See the PowerPoint presentation on www.myhealthprofessionskit.com for a video on the topic of a career in medical assisting.

ETYMOLOGY

Surgeon comes from a Latin word meaning *hand work*.

CHAPTER REVIEW EXERCISES

Test your knowledge of the chapter by completing these review exercises. Use the Answer Key at the end of the book to check your answers.

Anatomy and Physiology

Matching Exercise

Match each word or phrase to its description.

1. cholecystokinin
2. chyme
3. deglutition
4. enzyme
5. haustra
6. jejunum
7. lipase
8. lumen
9. mastication
10. meconium
11. omentum
12. parotid gland
13. rectum

_7_ Enzyme that breaks apart fats

_9_ The act of chewing

_12_ One of the three salivary glands

_1_ Hormone from the duodenum that stimulates the gallbladder to contract

_11_ Fatty sheet of peritoneum that supports the stomach

_13_ Last part of the large intestine

_10_ First feces of newborn infants

_6_ Second part of the small intestine

_4_ Substance that breaks the chemical bonds between molecules of food

_5_ Pouches in the mucosa of the large intestine

_3_ The act of swallowing

_8_ Open channel inside the intestines

_2_ Partially digested food and digestive enzymes in the stomach

Circle Exercise

Circle the correct word from the choices given.

1. The first part of the small intestine is the (**cecum, colon, (duodenum)**).
2. The process of having a bowel movement is known as (**(defecation)**, **emulsification, mastication**).
3. The part of the stomach that is closest to the esophagus is the (**body, (cardia), pylorus**).
4. What structure secretes a digestive enzyme? (**esophagus, pharynx, (salivary gland)**)
5. The digestive enzyme (**amylase, (hydrochloric acid), lipase**) is *not* secreted by the pancreas.
6. The S-shaped segment of colon is the (**jejunum, (sigmoid), transverse**).
7. Emulsification of fat globules in food is done by (**(bile), flatus, lactase**).

True or False Exercise

Indicate whether each statement is true or false by writing T or F on the line.

1. _T_ The stomach is superior to the small intestine.
2. _T_ The salivary glands and pancreas both secrete amylase.
3. _F_ The structure that comes after the duodenum is the ileum.
4. _T_ The colon is the longest part of the large intestine.
5. _F_ The appendix is considered to be part of the gastrointestinal system and the endocrine system.

6. _T___ Mucosa lines the gastrointestinal tract.

7. _F___ You can find villi in the large intestine.

8. _F___ Deglutition is waves of contractions that propel food through the GI tract.

9. _F___ The omentum carries food nutrients from the intestines to the liver.

10. _T___ The parotid gland is one of the salivary glands.

Sequencing Exercise

Beginning with food entering the mouth, write each structure of the gastrointestinal system in the order in which food moves through it.

Structure	Correct Order
anus	1. oral cavity
cecum	2. pharynx
colon	3. esophagus
duodenum	4. stomach
esophagus	5. duodenum
ileum	6. jejunum
jejunum	7. ileum
oral cavity	8. cecum
pharynx	9. colon
rectum	10. rectum
stomach	11. anus

Diseases and Conditions

Matching Exercise

Match each word or phrase to its description.

1. hematochezia
2. choledocholithiasis
3. incontinence
4. hematemesis
5. obstipation
6. cheilitis
7. hepatosplenomegaly
8. steatorrhea
9. melena
10. varices
11. hyperemesis gravidarum
12. adenocarcinoma
13. cirrhosis

_13__ Chronic liver disease with nodular liver

_9___ Dark, tar-like feces that contain old blood

_2___ Gallstones in the common bile duct

_6___ Inflammation of the lips

_7___ Enlargement of the liver and spleen

_8___ Fatty feces and malabsorption of dietary fat

_12__ A type of stomach cancer

_1___ Blood in the feces

_11__ Excessive vomiting of pregnancy

_5___ Severe constipation

_3___ Inability to control bowel movements

_4___ Vomiting blood

_10__ Swollen veins in the esophagus

True or False Exercise

Indicate whether each statement is true or false by writing T or F on the line.

1. T____ Indigestion is known by the medical name *dyspepsia*.
2. F____ A hiatal hernia occurs in the groin.
3. T____ A peptic ulcer is an ulcer in the esophagus, stomach, or duodenum.
4. F____ An ileus is an abnormal fibrous band that forms between two organs following abdominal surgery.
5. F____ A ruptured appendix can cause diverticulosis.
6. T____ Hepatoma is another name for liver cancer.
7. T____ Pancreatitis can occur when a gallstone blocks the common bile duct near the duodenum.

Laboratory, Radiology, Surgery, and Drugs

Fill in the Blank Exercise

Fill in the blank with the correct word from the word list.

albumin	cholangiography	nasogastric tube	sonogram
antiemetic	herniorrhaphy	ova and parasites	stoma
barium swallow	laxative		

1. Surgically created opening like a mouth *stoma*
2. A medicine used to treat vomiting *antiemetic*
3. Major protein molecule in the blood *albumin*
4. Eggs and worms in the GI tract *ova and parasites*
5. Radiologic procedure that uses contrast dye to show the bile ducts *cholangiography*
6. An ultrasound is also known as a *sonogram*
7. Another name for an upper GI series *barium swallow*
8. Provides a temporary way to feed a patient *nasogastric tube*
9. Procedure that sutures a weak area in the abdominal wall that protrudes outward *herniorrhaphy*
10. A drug used to treat constipation *laxative*

Circle Exercise

Circle the correct word from the choices given.

1. The words *donor* and *recipient* are associated with this operative procedure: (**gastroplasty,** **liver transplantation,** **polypectomy**)
2. A gallbladder ultrasound is also known as a/an (**amylase test, ERCP, sonogram**)
3. Surgical removal of the gallbladder is known as a (**cholecystectomy, colectomy, colostomy**).
4. All of these are types of feeding tubes *except* (**colostomy, gastrostromy, jejunostomy**).
5. Gastroplasty is a popular surgery to treat (**colon polyps, heartburn, obesity**).
6. ALT is the newer name for the lab test (**albumin, CBD, SGPT**).
7. *Helicobacter pylori* causes what test to be positive? (**CLO, colonoscopy, gastric analysis**)
8. A/an (**anastomosis, endoscopy, laparotomy**) uses a long abdominal incision to explore the abdominal cavity.
9. The surgical procedure done to treat stomach cancer is a (**gastrectomy, gastroplasty, gastroscopy**).

Building Medical Words

Review the Combining Forms Exercise, Combining Form and Suffix Exercise, Prefix Exercise, and Multiple Combining Forms and Suffix Exercise that you already completed in the anatomy section on pages 103–105.

Combining Forms Exercise

Before you build gastrointestinal words, review these additional combining forms. Next to each combining form, write its medical meaning. The first one has been done for you.

Combining Form	Medical Meaning		Combining Form	Medical Meaning
1. anastom/o-	create an opening between two structures		16. log/o-	word; the study of
2. cheil/o-	lip		17. obstip/o-	severe constipation
3. cirrh/o-	yellow		18. obstruct/o-	blocked by a barrier
4. constip/o-	compacted feces		19. omphal/o-	umbilicus; navel
5. contin/o-	hold together		20. orex/o-	appetite
6. diverticul/o-	diverticulum		21. pept/o-	digestion
7. emet/o-	to vomit		22. perfor/o-	to have an opening
8. hemat/o-	blood		23. phag/o-	eating; swallowing
9. hemorrhoid/o-	hemorrhoid		24. polyp/o-	polyp
10. herni/o-	hernia		25. pyr/o-	fire; burning
11. hiat/o-	gap; opening		26. regurgitat/o-	flow backward
12. inguin/o-	groin		27. rotat/o	rotate
13. intussuscep/o-	to receive within		28. splen/o-	spleen
14. jaund/o-	yellow		29. steat/o-	fat
15. lith/o-	stone		30. umbilic/o-	umbilicus; navel

Related Combining Forms Exercise

Write the combining forms on the line provided. (Hint: See the It's Greek to Me feature box.)

1. Two combining forms that mean *fats*. steat/o-, lip/o-
2. Two combining forms that mean *intestine*. enter/o-, intestin/o-
3. Two combining forms that mean *tongue*. gloss/o-, lingu/o-
4. Four combining forms that mean *abdomen*. celi/o-, abdomen/o-, lapar/o-, or ventr/o-
5. Three combining forms that mean *bile duct*. cholangi/o-, bili/o-, choledoch/o-

Dividing Medical Words

Separate these words into their component parts (prefix, combining form, suffix). Note: Some words do not contain all three word parts. The first one has been done for you.

Medical Word	Prefix	Combining Form	Suffix	Medical Word	Prefix	Combining Form	Suffix
1. anorexia	an-	orex/o-	-ia	5. hematemesis		hemat/o-	-emesis
2. appendectomy		append/o-	-ectomy	6. hepatomegaly		hepat/o-	-megaly
3. mesenteric		mesenter/o-	-ic	7. herniorrhaphy		herni/o-	-rrhaphy
4. dysphagia	dys-	phag/o-	-ia	8. sublingual	sub-	lingu/o-	-al

Combining Form and Suffix Exercise

Read the definition of the medical word. Select the correct suffix from the Suffix List. Select the correct combining form from the Combining Form List. Build the medical word and write it on the line. Be sure to check your spelling. The first one has been done for you.

SUFFIX LIST

-ation (a process; being or having)
-cele (hernia)
-ectomy (surgical excision)
-emesis (condition of vomiting)
-gram (a record or picture)
-itis (inflammation of; infection of)
-lith (stone)
-megaly (enlargement)
-oma (tumor; mass)
-osis (condition; abnormal condition; process)
-pathy (disease; suffering)
-rrhaphy (procedure of suturing)
-scope (instrument used to examine)
-scopy (process of using an instrument to examine)
-stomy (surgically created opening)
-tomy (process of cutting or making an incision)

COMBINING FORM LIST

anastom/o- (create an opening between two structures)
appendic/o- (appendix)
append/o- (appendix)
cholangi/o- (bile duct)
cholecyst/o- (gallbladder)
cirrh/o- (yellow)
col/o- (colon)
constip/o- (compacted feces)
diverticul/o- (diverticulum)
enter/o- (intestine)

gastr/o- (stomach)
gloss/o- (tongue)
hemat/o- (blood)
hemorrhoid/o- (hemorrhoid)
hepat/o- (liver)
herni/o- (hernia)
lapar/o- (abdomen)
polyp/o- (polyp)
rect/o- (rectum)
sial/o- (saliva; salivary gland)
sigmoid/o- (sigmoid colon)

Definition of the Medical Word | Build the Medical Word

1. Being or having compacted feces — constipation
2. Inflammation or infection of the stomach — gastritis
3. Condition of vomiting of blood — hematemesis
4. Enlargement of the liver — hepatomegaly
5. Inflammation or infection of the appendix — appendicitis
6. Disease of the intestine — enteropathy
7. Surgical excision of the gallbladder — cholecystectomy
8. Abnormal condition (of having) diverticula — diverticulosis
9. Process of cutting or making an incision into the abdomen — laparotomy
10. Inflammation or infection of the liver — hepatitis
11. Surgical excision of a polyp — polypectomy
12. Tumor of the liver — hepatoma
13. Surgical excision of the appendix — appendectomy
14. Procedure of suturing a hernia — herniorrhaphy
15. Process of using an instrument to examine the sigmoid colon — sigmoidoscopy
16. Inflammation or infection of the gallbladder — cholecystitis
17. Create an opening between two structures (such as the intestine) — anastomosis
18. Inflammation or infection of the tongue — glossitis
19. Surgically created opening in the colon — colostomy
20. Instrument used to examine (the inside of) the abdomen — laparoscope

Definition of the Medical Word

Build the Medical Word

21. Surgical excision of hemorrhoids   hemorrhoidectomy

22. Hernia in the rectum   rectocele

23. Stone in a salivary gland   sialolith

24. Abnormal condition (of the liver that causes the skin to be) yellow   cirrhosis

25. A record or (x-ray) picture of the bile ducts   cholangiogram

Prefix Exercise

Read the definition of the medical word. Look at the medical word or partial word that is given (it already contains a combining form and a suffix.) Select the correct prefix from the Prefix List and write it on the blank line. Then build the medical word and write it on the line. Be sure to check your spelling. The first one has been done for you.

PREFIX LIST

an- (without; not)
anti- (against)
dys- (painful; difficult; abnormal)
im- (not)

in- (in; within; not)
mal- (bad; inadequate)
poly- (many; much)

sub- (below; underneath; less than)
trans- (across; through)

Definition of the Medical Word	Prefix	Word or Partial Word	Build the Medical Word
1. Condition of not digesting	in-	digestion	indigestion
2. Condition of (being) without an appetite	an-	orexia	anorexia
3. Condition of painful or abnormal digestion	dys-	pepsia	dyspepsia
4. Condition of bad rotation (of the intestine)	mal-	rotation	malrotation
5. Pertaining to underneath the tongue	sub-	lingual	sublingual
6. Condition of much eating	poly-	phagia	polyphagia
7. Pertaining to (a drug that is) against vomiting	anti-	emetic	antiemetic
8. Condition of painful or difficult eating or swallowing	dys-	phagia	dysphagia
9. Pertaining to not having an opening (at the anus)	im-	perforate	imperforate
10. State of not (being able to) hold together (feces in the rectum)	in-	continence	incontinence

Multiple Combining Forms and Suffix Exercise

Read the definition of the medical word. Select the correct suffix and combining forms. Then build the medical word and write it on the line. Be sure to check your spelling. The first one has been done for you.

SUFFIX LIST	COMBINING FORM LIST	
-al (pertaining to)	bili/o- (bile; gall)	hepat/o- (liver)
-ia (condition; state; thing)	chez/o- (to pass feces)	lapar/o- (abdomen)
-ic (pertaining to)	col/o- (colon)	lith/o- (stone)
-in (a substance)	choledoch/o- (common bile duct)	log/o- (word; the study of)
-ist (one who specializes in)	duoden/o- (duodenum)	nas/o- (nose)
-itis (inflammation of; infection of)	enter/o- (intestine)	rect/o- (rectum)
-megaly (enlargement)	esophag/o- (esophagus)	rub/o- (red)
-scopy (process of using an instrument to examine)	gastr/o- (stomach)	scop/o- (examine with an instrument)
	hemat/o- (blood)	splen/o- (spleen)
-tomy (process of cutting or making an incision)		

Definition of the Medical Word

Build the Medical Word

1. A substance (composed of) bile and (taken from blood cells that are) red

bilirubin

2. Process of using an instrument to examine the esophagus, stomach, and duodenum

esophagogastroduodenoscopy

3. Inflammation or infection of the stomach and intestine

gastroenteritis

4. Enlargement of the liver and spleen

hepatosplenomegaly

5. Pertaining to (a tube that goes through) the nose (to) the stomach

nasogastric

6. Condition of blood (when you) pass feces

hematochezia

7. Pertaining to the colon and rectum

colorectal

8. One who specializes in stomach and intestines the study of

gastroenterologist

9. Process of cutting or making an incision into the common bile duct (to remove) a stone

choledocholithotomy

10. Process of using an instrument to examine (inside) the abdomen

laparoscopy

Abbreviations

Matching Exercise

Match each abbreviation to its description.

1. ALT	13	Also known as a barium swallow
2. C&S	1	SGPT was its former name
3. CBD	3	A duct that bile flows through
4. CLO test	4	Screening test for *Helicobacter pylori*
5. GERD	8	Feeding tube from nose to stomach
6. LFTs	5	Stomach acid irritates the esophagus
7. N&V	6	Blood tests for hepatic function
8. NG	2	Tells which antibiotic drug a bacterium is sensitive to
9. NPO	11	Feeding tube surgically inserted in the stomach
10. O&P	7	Upset stomach and emesis
11. PEG	12	One of four abdominal quadrants
12. RUQ	9	Nothing by mouth
13. UGI	10	Test for worms and eggs of parasites in the feces

Applied Skills

Adjective Spelling Exercise

Read the noun and write the adjective form. Be sure to check your spelling. The first one has been done for you.

Noun	Adjective Form		Noun	Adjective Form
1. abdomen	abdominal		9. cecum	cecal
2. mouth	oral		10. appendix	appendiceal
3. pharynx	pharyngeal		11. colon	colonic
4. esophagus	esophageal		12. rectum	rectal
5. stomach	gastric		13. anus	anal
6. pylorus	pyloric		14. peritoneum	peritoneal
7. duodenum	duodenal		15. liver	hepatic
8. jejunum	jejunal		16. pancreas	pancreatic

Proofreading and Spelling Exercise

Read the following paragraph. Identify each misspelled medical word and write the correct spelling of it on the line provided.

Gastrointerology is the study of the digestive organs. Food moves into the pharinxy from the mouth and then down the esophogus. You won't develop diverticulee or hemorroids if you eat a high-fiber diet, but cholelithasis could still be a problem. If the lumin of your bowel is filled with polips, then you may need to have surgery. A rectoseel can affect the vagina in women. If you do not eat enough protein, the albumen level in your blood will be low.

1.	gastroenterology		6.	cholelithiasis
2.	pharynx		7.	lumen
3.	esophagus		8.	polyps
4.	diverticula		9.	rectocele
5.	hemorrhoids		10.	albumin

English and Medical Word Equivalents Exercise

For each English word, write its equivalent medical word. Be sure to check your spelling. The first one has been done for you.

English Word	Medical Word		English Word	Medical Word
1. belly	abdomen		8. indigestion	dyspepsia
2. belly button	umbilicus or navel		9. mouth	oral cavity
3. bowel, gut	intestine		10. piles	hemorrhoids
4. bowel movement	defecation or feces or stool		11. swallowing	deglutition
5. chewing	mastication		12. throat	pharynx
6. gas	flatus		13. throwing up	emesis
7. heartburn	pyrosis			

You Write the Medical Report

You are a healthcare professional interviewing a patient. Listen to the patient's statements and then enter them in the patient's medical record using medical words and phrases. Be sure to check your spelling. The first one has been done for you.

1. The patient says, "I can't explain it. I just don't seem to have any appetite at all for the past few weeks, and that's not like me at all."

   You write: The patient is complaining of _____ anorexia _____ that has been present for the past few weeks.

2. The patient says, "I had cancer of the colon in 2008 and they took out my colon and made this new opening in my abdomen."

   You write: The patient had cancer of the colon in 2008 and a _____ colostomy _____ was performed.

3. The patient says, "Oh that bug was going around and I caught it from my kids—you know that intestinal virus with nausea, vomiting, and diarrhea. I had it for 4 days."

   You write: The patient developed viral _____ gastroenteritis _____ with symptoms of nausea, vomiting, and diarrhea for 4 days.

4. The patient says, "I strain most times when I try to pass a stool, but it never gets really bad."

   You write: The patient reports that she has frequent episodes of _____ constipation _____, but denies having any _____ obstipation _____.

5. The patient says, "I don't want to but I know I am supposed to have one of those procedures where they use an instrument to look into your bowel, so I guess it's time to go."

   You write: The patient is apprehensive about having a _____ colonoscopy _____ performed, but is agreeable to my referring her for this procedure.

6. The patient says, "I went to see that doctor at the hospital who specializes in treating the GI system, and he said I have an ulcer."

   You write: The patient was seen by a _____ gastroenterologist _____ at the hospital who diagnosed her as having an ulcer.

7. The patient says, "This is an emergency. I have an old ulcer in my esophagus, but today I just started vomiting up blood. I know I am an alcoholic, and my liver has disease and my abdomen is all swollen up with fluid, too."

   You write: The patient has a history of an _____ esophageal _____ ulcer and today had an episode of _____ hematemesis _____. He has a past history of alcoholism with a diagnosis of _____ cirrhosis _____, and now has an enlarged abdomen with _____ ascites _____.

8. The patient says, "I have an acidy, irritated stomach with gas when I eat spicy foods."

   You write: The patient complains of _pyrosis (or gastritis)_ with _____ flatus _____ after eating spicy foods.

9. The patient says, "You know I have had these stones in my gallbladder that keep giving me trouble, so is it time for me to have them taken out?"

   You write: The patient has frequent bouts of _____ cholecystitis _____ and is now considering the surgical option of having a _____ cholecystectomy _____ done.

10. The patient says, "You know that past stroke I had. Well, I still have difficulty eating from that. I also lost weight and now my dentures don't fit right and they hurt when I eat."

    You write: The patient is complaining of _____ dysphagia _____ due to impairment from a past stroke and also weight loss that resulted in poorly fitting dentures that cause pain.

Medical Report Exercise

This exercise contains two related reports: a hospital Admission History and Physical Examination and a Pathology Report. Read both reports and answer the questions.

ADMISSION HISTORY AND PHYSICAL EXAMINATION

PATIENT NAME:	MARTINEZ, Javier
HOSPITAL NUMBER:	138-524-7193
DATE OF ADMISSION:	NOVEMBER 19, 20xx

HISTORY OF PRESENT ILLNESS

This is a 20-year-old Hispanic male who experienced severe abdominal pain beginning on the morning of admission. He was awakened at 6:00 A.M. by sharp pains in the stomach. Drinking a glass of milk, which usually helps this type of pain, was not effective. He also took his customary antacid, but with no relief. He went to college and ate lunch there and then developed nausea and vomiting. An hour later, he developed watery diarrhea with approximately 3–4 bowel movements over the next few hours. He denies any history of ulcerative colitis or Crohn's disease. By this evening, his pain was so severe that he came to the emergency room to be seen.

PHYSICAL EXAMINATION

Temperature 100.2, pulse 04, respiratory rate 30, blood pressure 132/88. He is alert and oriented, lying uncomfortably in bed. Abdominal examination: Abdomen is soft. There is rebound tenderness in the RLQ.

LABORATORY DATA

Labs drawn in the emergency room showed an elevated white blood cell count of 14.6. Bilirubin and amylase were within normal limits. Urinalysis was unremarkable.

IMPRESSION

Acute appendicitis.

DISCUSSION

A detailed discussion was carried out with the patient and his parents. The dangers of waiting and observing his condition were discussed as well as the indications, possible risks, complications, and alternatives to an appendectomy. They agree with the plan to perform an appendectomy, and the patient will be taken to the operating room shortly.

James R. Rodgers, M.D.

James R. Rodgers, M.D.

JRR/bjg
D: 11/19/xx
T: 11/19/xx

PATHOLOGY REPORT

PATIENT NAME: MARTINEZ, Javier

HOSPITAL NUMBER: 138-524-7193

DATE OF REPORT: NOVEMBER 19, 20xx

SPECIMEN: Appendix

GROSS EXAMINATION
The specimen identified as "appendix" is an inflamed, vermiform appendix with an attached piece of the mesoappendix. The appendix measures 6.5 cm in length and up to 1.3 cm in diameter. There is a yellow-gray exudate noted inside with marked hemorrhage of the mucosa. There is no evidence of tumor or fecalith.

PATHOLOGICAL DIAGNOSIS
Acute appendicitis.

Leona T. Parkins, M.D.

Leona T. Parkins, M.D.

LTP:rrg
D: 11/19/xx
T: 11/19/xx

Word Analysis Questions

1. The patient had sharp pains in his stomach. If you wanted to use the adjective form of *stomach,* you would say, "He had sharp _____gastric_____ pains."

2. Divide *appendicitis* into its two word parts and define each word part.

Word Part	Definition
appendic/o-	(appendix)
-itis	(inflammation of; infection of)

3. Divide *fecalith* into its two word parts and define each word part.

Word Part	Definition
fec/a-	(feces; stool)
-lith	(stone)

4. Where is the RLQ? In the right upper quadrant

5. What is the abbreviation for *nausea and vomiting*? N&V

Fact Finding Questions

1. What is the name of the category of drug that neutralizes acid in the stomach?

   antacid

2. What is another medical name for *vomiting*?

   emesis

3. Ulcerative colitis and Crohn's disease both affect which part of the gastrointestinal system?

   the colon

4. What does *vermiform* mean?

   <u>wormlike</u>

5. What is the medical word that means *surgical excision of the appendix*?

   <u>appendectomy</u>

6. According to the pathology report on the specimen removed during surgery, what was the patient's diagnosis?

   <u>accute appendicitis</u>

Critical Thinking Questions

1. The patient has taken milk and an antacid in the past for his stomach pains. This suggests he has a previous history of what disease condition? Circle the correct answer.

   (pyrosis)   **colon cancer**   **hemorrhoids**

2. Acute symptoms of nausea and vomiting with diarrhea might lead you to think that the patient has what disease? Circle the correct answer.

   jaundice   **hematochezia**   (gastroenteritis)

3. An elevated white blood cell count is associated with an infection. Where was the site of this patient's infection?

   <u>in the appendix</u>

4. The danger in waiting and observing the patient's condition was that he could develop a ruptured appendix that would lead to what condition? Circle the correct answer.

   (peritonitis)   **gastritis**   **cholecystitis**

5. The patient had a finding of "rebound tenderness" on the physical examination. Describe what the physician did to check for rebound tenderness.

   <u>To check for rebound tenderness, the physician presses on that area of the abdomen and then quickly removes the hand and releases the pressure.</u>

6. The patient's bilirubin was within normal limits. This tells you that he is not having any problems with which of these organs?

   stomach   (liver)   **pancreas**

7. The patient's amylase was within normal limits. This tells you that he is not having any problems with which of these organs?

   (pancreas)   **colon**   **esophagus**

On the Job Challenge Exercise

On the job, you will encounter new medical words. Practice your medical dictionary skills by looking up the medical words in bold and writing their definitions on the lines provided.

OFFICE CHART NOTE

This is a 68-year-old white female with episodic abdominal pain, some headaches, heartburn symptoms, **aerophagia** and **eructation**, obstipation, and **tenesmus**. The patient presented with a 3-day history of **singultus**, unrelieved by any medications. Her physical examination revealed **borborygmus** and a slightly tender abdomen, but no evidence of rebound.

---

1. aerophagia <u>condition (caused by) air that is swallowed (excessively)</u>

2. eructation <u>process of (air being) brought up (from the stomach), belching</u>

3. tenesmus <u>painful straining to have a stool</u>

4. singultus <u>hiccups</u>

5. borborygmus <u>a rumbling sound due to gas in the intestines</u>

Hearing Medical Words Exercise

You hear someone speaking the medical words given below. Read each pronunciation and then write the medical word it represents. Be sure to check your spelling. The first one has been done for you.

1. AN-oh-REK-see-ah   anorexia
2. ah-SY-teez   ascites
3. KOH-lee-sis-TY-tis   cholecystitis
4. sih-ROH-sis   cirrhosis
5. koh-LAWS-toh-mee   colostomy
6. GAS-troh-EN-ter-EYE-tis   gastroenteritis
7. HER-nee-OR-ah-fee   herniorrhaphy
8. LAP-ah-RAW-toh-mee   laparotomy
9. NAY-zoh-GAS-trik   nasogastric
10. SIG-moy-DAWS-koh-pee   sigmoidoscopy

Pronunciation Exercise

Read the medical word that is given. Then review the syllables in the pronunciation. Circle the primary (main) accented syllable. The first one has been done for you.

1. gastric (**gas**-trik)
2. appendicitis (ah-pen-dih-**sy**-tis)
3. cholecystectomy (koh-lee-sis-**tek**-toh-mee)
4. dysphagia (dis-**fay**-jee-ah)
5. gastroenterologist (gas-troh-en-ter-**awl**-oh-jist)
6. gastrointestinal (gas-troh-in-**tes**-tih-nal)
7. hepatic (heh-**pat**-ik)
8. hepatitis (hep-ah-**ty**-tis)
9. hepatosplenomegaly (hep-ah-toh-splen-oh-**meg**-ah-lee)
10. peristalsis (pair-ih-**stal**-sis)

Multimedia Preview

Immerse yourself in a variety of activities inside Medical Terminology Interactive. Getting there is simple:

1. Click on www.myhealthprofessionskit.com.
2. Select "Medical Terminology" from the choice of disciplines.
3. First-time users must create an account using the scratch-off code on the inside front cover of this book.
4. Find this book and log in using your username and password.
5. Click on Medical Terminology Interactive.
6. Take the elevator to the 3rd Floor to begin your virtual exploration of this chapter!

Racing Pulse　Don't miss a beat! Your challenge is to answer quiz show questions to top the computer. With each correct answer you earn a spin of the dial which tells you how many pulses to advance. First around the body is a winner.

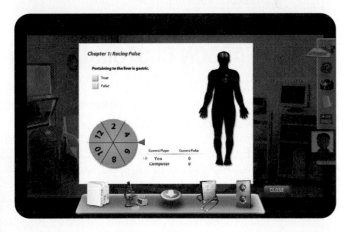

Spelling Challenge　Would you be the winner in a medical terminology spelling bee? Test your skills, listen to a pronounced medical word and then attempt to spell it correctly.

PEARSON
myhealthprofessionskit

CUSTOMIZE THIS BOOK?

NOW the Power is in Your Hands

Create your ideal text by assembling content from this book or combining content from this and other Pearson titles. You can even add your own material or content from other sources! Just click on **www.pearsoncustom.com**, type in the keyword "allied health," and select the Custom Library.

PEARSON CUSTOM LIBRARY OFFERS:

- **FLEXIBILITY** Choose only the content you need from one or more titles. Sequence them based on your course syllabus.

- **USE OF OUTSIDE MATERIALS** Up to 20% can come from outside sources. We'll secure the permissions.

- **COST SAVINGS** Students pay only for the content you choose.

- **QUALITY FINISHED PRODUCT** Your book wil be professionally designed and will have sequential pagination and an index.

- **PERSONALIZATION OPTIONS** You may wish to have your name, your course, and your school printed on the cover.

- **COMPLIMENTARY PREVIEWS** See your book before you decide to adopt! Build your book and then you can request a preview copy.

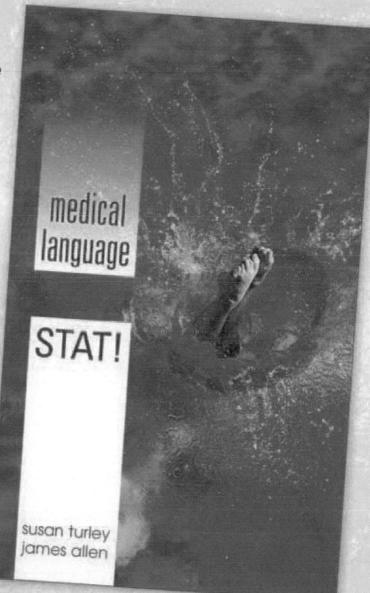